STRAW BALE GARDENS *Complete*

BREAKTHROUGH VEGETABLE GARDENING METHOD

JOEL KARSTEN

MINNEAPOLIS, MINNESOTA

First published in 2015 by Cool Springs Press, an imprint of Quarto Publishing Group USA Inc.,
400 First Avenue North, Suite 400, Minneapolis, MN 55401

Cool Springs Press titles are also available at discounts in bulk quantity for industrial or sales-promotional use. For details write to Special Sales Manager at Quarto Publishing Group USA Inc., 400 First Avenue North, Suite 400, Minneapolis, MN 55401 USA. To find out more about our books, visit us online at www.coolspringspress.com.

Library of Congress Control Number: 2014955422

ISBN: 978-1-59186-907-8

Acquisitions Editor: Mark Johanson
Art Director: Cindy Samargia Laun
Cover Design: Erin Seaward-Hiatt
Book Design: Pauline Molinari
Layout: Pauline Molinari and Rebecca Pagel
Photography: Tracy Walsh
Illustration: Pam Powell and Bill Kersey

Printed in China
10 9 8 7 6 5 4 3 2

Dedication

This book is dedicated to the one true love of my life, Patty, without whom I would have no sunny days.

Contents

Introduction

IT SEEMS LIKE I'VE TOLD THE STORY of Straw Bale Gardening a million times over the years, to audiences big and small all over the world. But I never get tired of it. It's a good story and it keeps getting better, in large part because my method is young and always evolving and improving. That's also the reason we chose to come out with a new edition of my book so soon after the first *Straw Bale Gardens* was published just a couple of years ago. The tens of thousands of gardeners who've decided to give my SBG technique a try are an enthusiastic group, and I get an enormous amount of direct feedback and many, many questions. I listen, and I'm constantly working to expand the techniques in ways that address the most common concerns people have. This has resulted in some very exciting additions to the information and advice I have offered before. The basics haven't changed at all, but I think you'll find several new ideas that make the SBG method more accessible and more practical for even more people.

When folks hear me describe Straw Bale Gardening for the first time, the reaction is fairly predictable. At first, they wonder how it works and they ask questions like "How to you get the dirt into the bales?" But then there is a moment where the light goes on and they understand that you don't use dirt at all: it's the straw itself that feeds the plants. I love the way you can see the sudden look of understanding when people smile and nod and even shake their heads in a kind of amazement. It might be what I love most about teaching the SBG method.

Once people get it, the questions usually come in waves. Where do you get the bales? Can you make an organic SBG? What about planting seeds? Can I put an SBG on my deck or driveway? Does it really work? In this second edition of my book I've done my best to provide new answers and solutions. Even if you are one of the more than 100,000 people who have read the first book cover to cover, I think you'll find some great new information in *Straw Bale Gardens Complete* that will make your SBG experience even more productive and efficient.

—Joel

The Author as a farmboy, working hard and dreaming up new ways of doing things.

The Straw Bale Gardening Story II

Everyone has heard it said that "necessity is the mother of invention," and I must agree. It was just after graduating from college, and hours after buying my first house, that I discovered my new home was surrounded with construction fill. Instead of the fertile farmland I grew up on, I found only clay, gravel, rocks, and old bricks that had been graded, compacted, and frosted with an inch of "blackish" topsoil. Anyone with even a rudimentary working knowledge of growing plants could decipher the cards I'd been dealt. Planting anything in this "soil" would require a backhoe, a couple of months with a pick axe, and several truck-loads of good quality compost to amend the "concrete" into a state where it might actually produce something. Rescuing this soil would be very expensive, so for a young, new homeowner with college loans to pay, it wasn't an option.

While I didn't have much money, I did have a fresh Bachelor of Science in Horticulture degree from the University of Minnesota, as well as some distinct memories of growing up on a small farm. There, we always seemed to have a few broken bales of straw that would get piled up along the side of the barn. After a few months of decomposing, the biggest, greenest, healthiest thistles on the whole farm would spring up from these bales. I wondered, even as a young boy, why the healthiest looking weeds were always the ones growing out of these old bales, but as a recent horticulture student I now knew. In my exhaustive study of soils, composting, plant physiology, and all things horticulture, I found that most mysteries, including why weeds grow in bales, can be explained by science—microbial soil science, to be exact. The old bales, I deduced, were composting inside, creating brand new soil. This provided a phenomenal growing environment for weeds. So why, then, couldn't I use bales of straw to grow vegetables? I decided to explore the question and I'll say it again: "necessity is the mother of invention." If I had been able to come up with $200 to build raised beds instead, you might well be reading a mystery novel right now, instead of this book called *Straw Bale Gardens Complete.*

The system I now like to call "SBG" wasn't an instant success, unless you consider 15 years of experimenting and perfecting a method to be instant success. It's not as simple as it might seem to some onlookers and many would-be bale-gardeners who don't bother to learn the right method. "Well, you just buy a bale of straw and dig out the inside and put in a little dirt and then drop in the plants," they conclude, "and Shazam! You have a garden." Not exactly. I've seen what happens when it's done this way, and it's a disaster. The plants starve to death and the dirt brings in weed seeds and disease we are trying to avoid.

Opposite: One of the test gardens in my own backyard. Over the years some of my neighbors may have wondered about my experiments, and it's hard to blame them.

Because the straw bale generates heat as the straw decomposes, a Straw Bale Garden can get a head start in planting and yield ripe tomatoes weeks before the other gardens in town.

The truth is that my method isn't really very complicated. The simplicity of the method, and the foolproof techniques I've developed, make vegetable gardening about as simple as following a recipe for baking cookies. You can deviate a little bit here and there, but if you want to be successful, make sure you adhere to the basics, or you'll end up with a garden that only disappoints.

Step One: Set aside the skepticism

The fact is, growing vegetables in straw bales is a very radical idea to traditional gardeners and even folks who have tried other out-of-the-ground strategies, like container gardening and raised bed gardening. You naturally encounter some serious skepticism when you tell these people that you've invented a method that: takes 75 percent less time; uses less water; involves less bending; requires less pesticide and no weeding; and, on top of that, can be done anywhere, even on a rooftop without using any soil at all. Then, add that it can be done on a shoestring budget, and you can't blame them if it sounds too good to be true.

"That's impossible...vegetables require nutrients...nutrients are only available in the soil, so how can crops be as productive or as nutritious if they are not grown in the soil?" is a typical objection I hear. Once they listen to my explanation, read the book or hear my seminar, however, the skepticism subsides a bit. The real proof, though, is in the pudding. They need to try it for themselves, and this is where the real foundation of the Straw Bale Gardening movement has been built.

Over the years I have told hundreds of audiences, "When you first put bales of straw in your yard, you are going to get some very funny looks!" But, I like to add, when you start a bale garden you will immediately become a teacher, and after a year or two you'll transition into a preacher. You will have to answer questions, explain what you're doing, and how this Straw Bale Gardening method actually works.

Because they've never done it, many first-time Straw Balers are also skeptical. But if they follow the method they become convinced. Not every single seed will sprout, and not every single plant will thrive, but overall the garden will provide many great successes and yield even greater satisfaction and enjoyment. Even those who have never grown a single thing discover that they can have a wonderful garden. It isn't necessary to grow a huge garden to be successful; I've seen many one-bale gardeners with smiles from cheek to cheek, even bragging a bit about their accomplishments.

As more and more people have tried and succeeded with Straw Bale Gardening, the movement has grow–rapidly. It's basically word-of-mouth advertising. Neighbors, friends, coworkers, and the random people who happen to strike up a conversation in line next to a successful Straw Bale Gardener, are seeing and hearing that it works and they decide to give it a try. Most find the simplicity to be appealing, and the no-weeding benefit gets a lot of attention, too. So does that fact that you can plant three or four weeks earlier in a bale than in the ground. But whatever reason draws the most interest, I've found that it's not my evangelizing or even a book that has sold tens of thousands on the idea; it is simply those who have done it and are true "Bale-ievers" (my affectionate name for Straw Bale Gardening believers).

The SBG Phenomenon

Since the first edition of *Straw Bale Gardens* hit the shelves, there has been a whirlwind of excitement and frenzy for me, and a bit of an earthquake within the gardening establishment. A *New York Times* garden writer, Michael Tortorello, read my book and came by my house one day to learn more about my method and about me. His resulting article was published on March 20, 2013, on a full page in the *New York Times*. Fortunately he gave rave reviews, calling my method "revolutionary." He also interviewed other gardeners who had tried my SBG method, and they all concurred that they loved it. I had no idea at the time what it meant to have a full page "book review" in the *New York Times*.

The morning when the *NYT* article was published I was sitting in my kitchen sipping on my coffee when my phone rang. To my surprise, it was a lovely woman with a very Spanish accent calling from Madrid, Spain. She was astonished that I would answer my phone, and explained that she had just read the *NYT* article and visited my website. There, she found my phone number and decided she was so excited to try this method that she would call and try to ask a few more questions. I answered her questions and we had a lovely chat, and then she concluded by once again telling me how amazed she was that I would actually answer her phone call. I told her, "I would have simply let my secretary answer the call, except…I don't have a secretary," and we had a good laugh together and she signed off.

That call was just a sign of what was to come. In the weeks that followed, the *NYT* article was reprinted in dozens of newspapers around the world, generating inquiries from international gardening magazines and many foreign newspapers. The media attention grew

Home and Garden shows, Flower shows, Healthy Living shows…you name it and I have probably given a presentation at one or more locations around the country. I love to see people get excited about growing a garden. The reactions I get are often as if I've just turned on a light bulb in the minds of many in the audience.

Straw Bale Garden Education Day at the Minnesota State Fair has become a popular event every spring. If you're in the area join us for a fun day of Straw Bale Garden discussion, and pick up some bales fresh from the farm, if there are any left when you get there!

like a tidal wave, with an Associated Press article that was reprinted in hundreds of newspapers. Soon after, a Reuters Newswire Article hit the press, and requests for interviews from radio, print, bloggers, podcasters, websites, and magazines came in hourly, and consumed my entire daily schedule. I was booked to speak at Home and Garden shows around the country, getting the largest audiences in many cases. More people were interested in Straw Bale Gardening than the big name television personalities who were supposed to be the main attractions. I was asked by the organizers of the Epcot International Flower and Garden Show to come to speak at Disney's amazing Epcot Center for three days during their annual show. It was such a wonderful experience, with so much interest there that they actually sold all the copies of my book they had ordered after just my first presentation, and I had five more to give.

It was not long before SBG truly went international. In the fall of 2013 I was lucky enough to attend the International Garden Festival at Chaumond, in the Loire Valley, France. There, several friends and fans of the Straw Bale Gardening method had constructed a display garden that demonstrated the SBG way to grow vegetables. It wasn't a simple garden layout like most vegetable gardens. It was an elaborate, artful creation with raised elevations, pathways, and a host of thriving crops. Their garden design was selected from among thousands of submissions made by landscape designers and artists from all over the world. Even more impressive, when we met the exhibition director she told us that in the 21 years they had been holding the exhibition, she "could not recall a garden which had generated more interest than the Straw Bale Garden."

It has been amazing and gratifying to see how the French have embraced the technique, as have many other Europeans, including Germans, the Dutch, the Spanish, the Danish, and even the Estonians. The book has now been translated into these and other foreign languages. Then, in September 2014, Straw Bale Gardens (I guess I should say *Le jardinage sur bottes de paille*) received the P.J. Redouté award, which is the highest achievement for Horticulture Books in France. I have many people to thank for the support they've offered to help make *Straw Bale Gardens* so successful all over the world.

Created by Pierre Marie Tricaud, Laurence Tricaud, Emmanuel Taillard and Pascale Marq, who were the four principle builders of the 2013 Straw Bale Garden installation at the International Garden Festival at Chaumont in the Loire Valley of France. It was spectacular and created world-wide buzz with over 400,000 international visitors over a six-month period.

There's no place like home

Although the concept has been embraced internationally, there is no denying that Straw Bale Gardening has reached its highest penetration in my local community around the Minneapolis and Saint Paul, Minnesota, metro areas. I have held an event each spring called "Straw Bale Garden Education Day" at the Minnesota State Fair Grounds, and

SBG INSTRUCTORS

Since my first book was published, the invitations for me to speak and give seminars about Straw Bale Gardening have reached an almost unmanageable level. But because I hate to turn down anyone who is interested, I came up with a solution. Why not offer other Straw Bale Gardeners who have experience and a solid understanding of the method the opportunity to go out and speak to local groups? If someone has the desire and ability to stand up in front of a group of eager learners, why not make it possible for them to teach others how to be successful at straw bale gardening? Now we have launched a directory on our website with the names of Straw Bale Gardening instructors who are willing to come to local events in towns all over the world and speak about Straw Bale Gardening. These instructors can be easily located by the dots on our map or by zip code; just visit StrawBaleGardens.com and click on "Instructors." The instructors get some support from us to help them give an informative, professional quality presentation, and they often get paid to share their excitement with other garden clubs or civic groups in their part of the world.

it has been very well attended with thousands of new gardeners coming to learn about the technique and load their trucks and trailers with bales of straw. Because I am local, I have spoken to hundreds of garden clubs, groups, libraries, local garden shows, and it's created a bit of an unforeseen repercussion: with so many gardeners looking for straw bales, the local farmers can't easily keep up with the demand for bales, so the prices have gone up. It is a bit of a problem, but you'll discover later in this book that I have a few solutions for this, too.

The rapid growth for Straw Bale Gardening hasn't slowed, and will surely continue to explode as word spreads about the method. The overall gardening movement toward more locally and home grown food production is also a phenomenon that continues to grow. I encourage everyone to grow something; it is good for the soul. No one has ever spent a more productive and satisfying day than one spent working in their garden.

Has a soil-testing lab ever suggested that your gardening outfit should be a hazmat suit? Do you have a weed problem (and not that kind of weed problem)? One last question: Are you ready to learn about a transformative garden technology that could change your life — for less than $100?

—*Michael Tortorello,* New York Times

As popular as Straw Bale Gardening has become all over the world, its epicenter is still in my home state of Minnesota. A common Minnesota trailer is seen here hauling its limit of bales from the Minnesota State Fairgrounds.

Cross-section of a Straw Bale Garden (5-Bale)

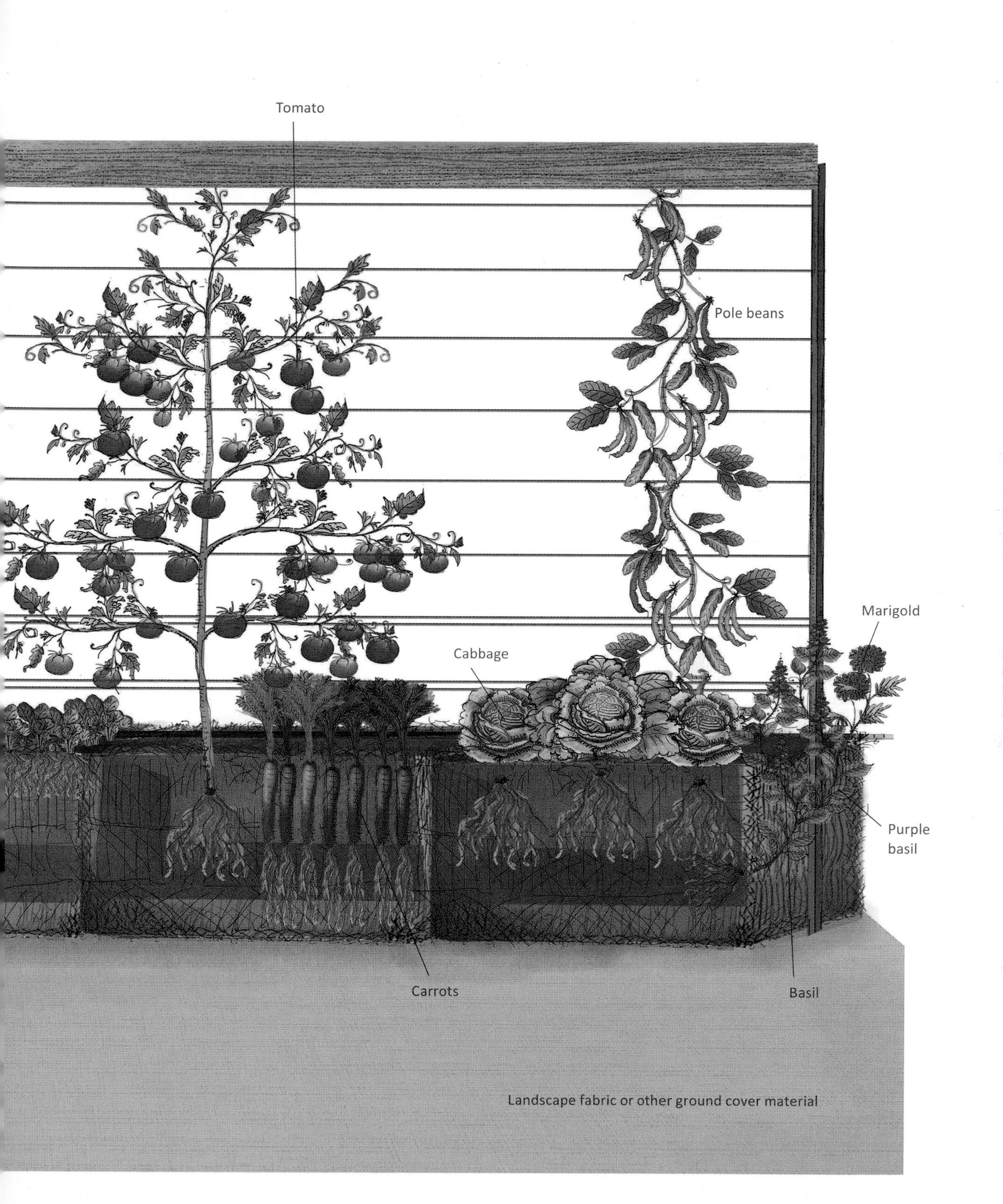
Tomato
Pole beans
Marigold
Cabbage
Purple basil
Carrots
Basil
Landscape fabric or other ground cover material

Straw Bale Gardening vs. Traditional Gardening

ATTRIBUTE	STRAW BALE GARDEN	TRADITIONAL SOIL GARDEN	CONTAINER/ RAISED BED GARDEN WITH MIX NOT SOIL
75% less labor	X	-	X (first year only)
Raised height, easy planting	X	-	X
No weeding	X	-	X (first year only)
Very low input/start-up cost	X	X	-
Extends the growing season	X	-	-
Higher germination on seeds	x	-	-
Predictable performance	X	-	X (first year only)
Impossible to overwater	X	-	-
Holds moisture well	X	-	-
Creates new media yearly	X	-	-
Easy to move location	X	-	-
Automated water daily is okay	X	-	X
No crop rotation needed	X	-	-
Can plant top and sides	X	-	-
Creates loads of A+ compost	X	-	-
Prevents disease issues	X	-	-
Prevents insect issues	X	-	-
Prevents rabbits/deer issues	X	-	-
Can be located anywhere	X	-	-
Prevents early season frost	X	-	-
No heavy work, tilling	X	-	-
No tools other than hand trowel	X	-	-
Warmed root zone at planting/seeding	X	-	-
Eliminates soil-borne disease	X	-	X (first year only)

Straw Bale Gardening in Four Steps

1. Place bales on any surface (driveways, rooftops, anywhere). Treat bales with high-nitrogen fertilizer (organic or conventional) to accelerate decomposition of straw inside bale. Water heavily for 12 to 18 days.

2. Plant seedlings and seeds directly in the bales. Seeds require a bed of potting soil to hold moisture atop the bale until germination. Heat generated by decomposing straw allows you to plant two to four weeks earlier than if you are planting in the ground. Continue watering.

3. Water, watch, and wait. No weeding.

4. Harvest. After the season, bales have turned into beautiful, clean compost for use in your other gardens. Next spring, repeat the process with fresh bales. Underground vegetables such as potatoes may be planted in second-year bales in some cases.

STRAW BALE GARDENING SUCCESSES

Isn't technology wonderful? Just a few years ago, straw bale gardens were rare and photos of them even rarer. Now, largely through the Internet and social media, I have been able to spread the word about Straw Bale Gardens to tens of thousands of curious people, and many of them have adopted the method. I know because they send pictures. If you have ever been on my website or my Facebook page, you've seen them. The first couple of years the photos weren't that great—pretty low quality and not really suitable for reproducing in a book. But over the last couple of years advancing digital camera and even cellphone camera technology has ramped up the photo quality a lot. I'll bet I've received over 1,000 excellent pictures that people have sent me of their own Straw Bale Gardens. On the following pages are a few of the ones I found most interesting and inspirational.

Mary maintains a very tidy looking garden filled with a wide variety of vegetables. She has always been one to try something new, but Straw Bale Gardening is something she plans to keep doing. Many of her neighbors are in "observation mode" this summer, next year she may inspire a whole new crop of SBGs in the neighborhood.

Even a tight location in a side-yard where space is limited befits a Straw Bale Garden set-up. This garden is quickly producing a bounty of produce that will continue throughout the season in this protected location.

Have you ever seen such beautiful cabbage? John has become a big proponent of Straw Bale Gardening, and said he gets one or two people stopping by every day with questions about his garden. He has become an expert in his second full year of using the SBG method, and is happy to pass along what he knows to those who are interested.

Not only does this Straw Bale Garden produce well, it also looks lovely and compliments the ornamental gardens that already existed nearby. Shallow tree roots do not affect the bales. In this garden they are within just a few feet of the trees, whereas a traditional garden in this location could be impossible with all the invasive roots.

Kate was originally trained as a landscape designer, but has become increasingly interested in edible landscaping and growing food, which led her to become a Certified Urban Farmer. She is now one of our Certified SBG instructors as well. Her garden is laid out very creatively to maximize production and add interest.

Above: A great example of a small garden in an urban location. Tomatoes are a "must grow" for many gardeners, and absolutely nothing grows better in a Straw Bale Garden than they do. This garden has many varieties of heirlooms in production; I think we should swing back in a month or so with a pail, or some bacon and lettuce!

Left: Tucked in along the south side of a row of spruce trees, this Straw Bale Garden is well on the way to making use of limited space where a traditional garden would never work. If surface roots from trees in your yard have prevented you from attempting a garden, put down a few bales and you'll be amazed at what you can grow.

A classic Straw Bale Garden configuration is displayed by this large SBG. Some gardeners choose to skip the posts that are driven at both ends of each bale row. In addition to supporting the trellis wires, the posts help keep the bales from slumping or shifting as they decompose.

From a Straw Bale Garden fan in New York: "I do the gardening at a restaurant in NY. This is our second year gardening in straw bales. We made a 'room' where visitors could sit and enjoy the vegetables and flowers."

This neat and tidy SBG grouping in France demonstrates that a Straw Bale Garden can have some rustic appeal even before the plants have grown up. This particular garden is located outside of an assisted living facility and the residents enjoy the great fresh vegetables it produces.

Above: For many people the space between their property and the street is wasted space. Not in this case—here it serves as the perfect spot for a single row of bales. In many cases the soil wouldn't be very productive in that spot anyway as it is often contaminated with road salt.

Left: Preparation is important for every garden, but after the bales are laid out and the trellis is built, most of the difficult work is done for the season. The results of your preparation will amaze you and impress those around you. Not a weed to be found anywhere in this garden!

Above: Setting up bales in a formerly overgrown plot is so much easier than trying to prep the soil for a garden planting in a situation like this. A traditional gardener would spend half their summer standing on their head pulling weeds, while this gardener won't pull a single weed.

Right: Trellis wires pulled from post to post, with a PVC pipe between the post tops, make a perfect set up for a variety of climbing plants, vines, or simply to hold vegetable plants laden with fruits upright and vertical.

Mixing plantings of flowers and vegetables in a garden can keep everyone interested. Flowers also keep the bees interested in your garden, helping to pollinate other veggies that might need help.

Front and center in this landscape, these gardeners decided to make their vegetable garden a topic of conversation by putting a configuration of bales in the center of the action. After having the usual amazing results, these folks have turned dozens of others into Straw Bale Gardening bale-ievers now as well. Experts now, after planting their first SBG only a year earlier.

So . . . you want to start a small Straw Bale Garden! A number of very large installations around the country have inspired hundreds. Several community gardens have converted entirely to bales, and several new community gardens have begun, based entirely around growing in Straw Bales.

Right: Using a double layer of bales can create two distinct planting "shelves" and make it much easier to plant and harvest without needing to bend over much at all.

Onions and other root crops require a loose and airy "soil," which is exactly what the inside of a straw bale provides. With lots of freshly developing compost inside, the bales have plentiful airspaces and this allows root crops to develop uninhibited.

This Straw Bale Garden in North Hollywood California is a testament to the enthusiasm many gardeners have for this method. Even a front yard can make a beautiful and productive garden, with just a couple dozen bales of straw.

Left: Summer bulbs such as these Dahlias are doing well in this bale at midseason and are being used as cut flowers for indoor display. The big advantage is that the bulbs are easily harvested and divided at the end of the season by simply opening the bale up, and no digging is required.

SBGs IN SMALL, URBAN AND UNUSUAL SPACES

ONE OF THE BIGGEST ADVANTAGES OF STRAW BALE GARDENING is that the gardener doesn't need soil and doesn't need to purchase a container, because the bale provides the media for growing and it also serves as its own container. If a regular garden is planned on a rooftop, the first call should be to a structural engineer, because it is assumed that many tons of heavy soil will be required to create planting beds. Not with a Straw Bale Garden, however; it will be significantly lighter in terms of overall weight. Each bale will absorb and hold about three to five gallons of water, which is going to more than double the dry weight once it gets soaking wet. Even so, it is still less than 1/3 the weight of the same volume of wet soil and thus less worrisome from an engineer's perspective and requires less heavy-lifting by the gardeners.

If the bales are being arranged on concrete or asphalt, there will be no worries about staining or damaging the surface, at least no more than a slight discoloration that any pressure sprayer can take care of when the bales are removed. Putting bales on a wood surface creates a bit more concern, as the constant moisture will cause damage to deck boards and likely ruin the stain or paint. You'll call and ask me to help you sand and paint your deck, and I will refer you back to this page in this book, with this caution: if you want to put a Straw

Opposite: One straw bale and some sunshine are all you need to get started enjoying Straw Bale Gardening. It's a good idea to set the bale on a protective mat, or you'll spend next summer sanding and staining your deck boards.

Diederik's garden on his rooftop in the Netherlands has gotten him excited about growing a garden. As a chef he knows the importance of using fresh herbs and vegetables when trying to create healthy and delicious dining experiences.

Bale Garden on a deck or other wood surface, you must put down a barrier underneath the bales to protect the wood. My suggestion is to use something that will allow for good air circulation underneath, not just plastic sheeting. Farm supply stores sell livestock stall mats, which are thick rubber mats with a waffle imprint on one side. Even the cheap hard plastic kiddie swimming pools work well for this; you can cut down the sides to lessen the visual impact. Allow one edge of the rubber or plastic barrier to hang over the edge of a raised deck or patio, thus guiding the excess water out and over the edge of the wood surface and off your downstairs' neighbor if you are in an apartment building. I've seen a number of tiny but lush gardens created in small spaces, and it amazes me how resourceful folks can be when it comes to using every available space.

If you want to put a garden on a solid surface like a patio or driveway, you won't be able to drive posts into the ground to create the trellis above the bales. Use standard length 2 x 4 studs to screw a trellis together like this one. This three-bale unit was made for under $15, and takes less than half an hour to build. You can use 1.5" PVC pipe to make a very functional free standing trellis, which lasts for a very long time.

For some urban folks, the look of an exposed bale of straw can be off-putting. Neighbors may ask if you are planning to bring goats into your backyard or garden space. Many interesting solutions exist to disguise the bale and even make it look splendid. I have taken to planting annual flowers in the sides of a bale, which really adds to the overall aesthetic. Several others who have observed the growth in popularity of Straw Bale Gardening have actually custom designed bale-sized planter boxes. Several models of these cedar wood boxes can be purchased online; plans to make your own are also available on our website. The boxes also help raise the height a bit more than the bales themselves, which, for those with physical limitations, can be an extra benefit.

Those who already know about Straw Bale Gardening know that one of its greatest benefits it is that is a raised-height garden. If you have physical limitations and require even more height, another great solution I learned from a kind and enthusiastic "seasoned" gentleman at one of my many presentations this past year, is the pallet-stack Straw Bale Garden. He used from 5 to 8 pallets depending on the crop he planned to grow on top. After the pallets are stacked to the desired height, make sure the top pallet has a solid surface; otherwise, the bale will sink down in between the slats later in the season as the bale decomposes. Then, simply condition and plant as normal, with every task now at waist height or higher. Pallets are cheap and often even free, if you are not in a hurry to find them by tomorrow. Depending on the length of your bales, it is likely you will get three bales on top of a standard pallet. Run a length of rope around the three bales to hold them all tightly together. You can plant anything in these bales, but if the crop gets too tall you might end up on a ladder picking tomatoes, so think ahead to what it will be once full-grown.

If you use the pallet-stack method and plant strawberry plants just remember to cover them with a layer of insulating straw or something over the winter. In cold climates, the above-ground roots will freeze and thaw often in the spring, which is usually what kills them. It is likely the berries will produce much better in the second season than in the first year, so be patient. Start a new one every year so you'll have a nice rotation. You'll likely need new bales after two seasons, so transplant the strawberries in early spring once the new bales are conditioned and ready to plant.

Stack up from 5 to 8 pallets, put three bales on top, and you now have a stand-up height garden where bending over isn't necessary at all. Be mindful of what you plant, or you may need a step ladder to reach up and harvest tomatoes.

This well-protected Straw Bale Garden is planted on an apartment balcony. Note the drainage pipe sticking out to direct water away from the downstairs neighbor. The bale rests on a raised wood platform so it gets great sun exposure as well.

Put a bale inside an attractive wood container and you can put it anywhere. This container is produced by Gronomics™ and custom-sized for a standard bale of straw.

This gardener needed her garden to be portable, so she could move it during the year as the sun changed positions. It doesn't get any more portable than a shopping cart does it?

COMMUNITY GARDENERS LOVE STRAW BALES

The soil which happens to exist on the community garden plot near you is usually what you're stuck with—unless you bring your own bales to the party. Community gardens have some drawbacks: weeds, diseases, insects, shared water spigots, and lots of pesky rules. Many of these issues can be solved or at least reduced by growing your community garden in bales. Community gardens in many locations around the country have reported great results with bales, some converting entirely to the Straw Bale Gardening method.

While community gardening rules vary greatly from one garden to another, some rules are difficult to deviate from. One common rule is that you are not allowed to monopolize the use of the garden hose, so you will need to hand water daily during the heat of summer. This can be difficult for Straw Bale Gardeners, because we need consistency in water application. Your solution is a water storage barrel, mounted on top of a waist-high table, to gravity-feed water through a drip irrigation system to up to ten bales using a battery powered hose end timer to control the flow. If you are so inclined, there are a number of solar powered 12 volt pond pumps on the market and programmable solar irrigation controllers which easily generate enough pressure to water up to 20 bales very efficiently. These systems may also work well for those with a summer cottage, for people who can only provide water to the garden during weekend visits. Fill the barrel with water in between those times and the system will water for you, using only solar power.

Community gardens can bring community insects and diseases, and sometimes the soil can be depleted, overused, or filled with weed seeds. Other rules may prevent you from leaving posts in the ground at the end of the season or may require you to leave nothing behind after the season, which can make Straw Bale Gardening more difficult. A wonderful new movement that I am a big fan of is being led by SharedDirt.com, a non-profit website seeking to help match land owners with nearby gardeners. The parties agree to share production and costs from their gardening efforts as compensation for the use of the land and water. The website makes it easy to find a local landowner willing to host a garden, so if you are looking for a place to start gardening, you might want to check it out.

The Kearny Community Garden in Kearney, NJ.

Straw

THE REASON COWS MOO AND PIGS OINK

STRAW IS A VERY VERSATILE material with many uses in addition to gardens. Archery targets, decoration and insulation are just a few of the ways we incorporate straw into our lives. But the most important use for straw today is as a bedding material for livestock, and for this use the straw must be dry. Only dry straw will absorb the moisture generated by pigs, cows, horses or chickens and hold that moisture inside the stems of the straw stalks. A little piece of straw trivia: Most livestock will not eat straw, and even if they did, it wouldn't do much for their diet, as it has very little nutritional value.

The farmer (or the farmer's kid) has the task of gathering the wet straw, removing it from the barn stalls, and then transporting it to the field in a manure spreader to be used as fertilizer that gets plowed into the soil. Using straw to maintain dry barn stalls prevents the spread of disease by halting the growth of bacteria, fungus and mold that can be harmful to livestock. Young livestock benefit the most from a deep layer of straw in their pens because they are especially vulnerable to bacteria, fungus, mold and viruses. If you listen closely after a farmer finishes bedding a cow's pen or a sow's stall with fresh dry straw, you just might hear the warm, dry animal give a little moo or oink to say thank you for the clean straw.

Breaking open a bale of straw for a new mother cow and her calf or for a sow and her litter is like putting fresh sheets on their bed. Straw has an amazing ability to absorb moisture and almost magically wick it away.

Opposite: A dry bale of straw is a $3 asset to a farmer, while a wet bale quickly becomes a liability worth nothing.

HOW THEY GET STRAW

When small grain crops like wheat are ready to harvest, the plant is cut off near the ground, and the seeds are removed inside the combine harvester via a complicated mechanism that separates the seeds from the stems (or the wheat from the chaff, as the saying goes). The nutrients are in the seeds harvested from the oats, wheat or barley, and they are collected in trailers as the harvester proceeds through the field. Most are sold to make oatmeal, wheat flour and all the thousands of foods that small grains are used to make. The bread you had for breakfast this morning likely came from one or more of the small grains grown in abundance by American farmers every year. The plants stalks are flung out the back of the combine harvester and left as a byproduct of the harvested grain. Then, a baling machine goes out into the field and sweeps up the stalks, packing them into tight round or rectangular bales for collection and transport.

Bale straw is shaped like drinking straws; the hollow stems wick water efficiently.

Tall buildings cause confusion, it seems

Hay and straw frequently are confused. I'm not exactly sure why this happens, but it could be because of the old Christmas carol "Away in a Manger." Remember the part where it says, "the little Lord Jesus, asleep on the hay?" For this reason, people have referred to the yellow colored straw used in every nativity scene since then, as hay. It isn't hay; hay is green, more coarse and wiry than straw, and hay wouldn't make a very soft bed. This famous manger may have had hay in it initially, but I can assure you that Mary would have wanted a softer bed for her baby, and she would have told Joseph to put straw in that manger instead. I wish I had a nickel for every time someone has asked me "Isn't straw the same thing as hay?" No. The answer is no, they are not at all the same thing. The aforementioned manger was likely filled with straw, not hay, because animals (and people) would most likely choose to sleep on straw. But I guess straw didn't rhyme, or maybe the song writer was a city kid who didn't know the difference. Hay and straw refer to different species of plants entirely, as different as a cat from a dog. Hay is usually baled grass or alfalfa and is green in color and is fodder for livestock, while straw is yellow or golden with little nutritional value but works well as bedding material for livestock. The confusion seems to increase the closer one gets to tall buildings. To a farm kid, the difference between hay and straw is obvious, like the difference to a city kid between a commuter train and a metro bus.

While it seems natural and intuitive to know they are different, and while the two have distinctly different uses, they could be confused easily if you weren't paying attention. They are about the same shape and size, and cost about the same depending on where you load, so in many ways they could be easily mistaken, especially if one didn't know for sure where they came from. If you start out with the wrong one, you'll end up wasting a couple bucks, in a place you really don't want to be.

Straw comes from one of the cereal small-grain plants. Most common are oats, wheat, barley, rice, flax and rye. The seeds are harvested and the stalks are baled up as a byproduct and used primarily as bedding material.

Straw bales or straw sponges?

The stalks of the small-grain plants have a unique physiology that allows them to be super absorbent. If one looks carefully it is easy to see that the stalks of straw are hollow inside, with a very narrow inside "tube." When the end of this narrow cylinder comes into contact with a droplet of water, there is a simple principle of physics called capillary action that causes the water droplet to climb inside the narrow tube. Once inside, the moisture is trapped due to another basic principle called adhesion, which is a force that holds one molecule of water to another. This force does not allow the water to run back out of the cylinder because it cannot break the surface tension (adhesive force) of the water droplet at the end of the cylinder. The water must evaporate out of that cylinder in order to dissipate.

This unique characteristic gives straw an extraordinary water-holding capacity. If one observes a nurse administering a blood test, it is easier to see how this principle of physics is demonstrated. The nurse touches the glass capillary tube to the droplet of blood on your finger and the blood quickly climbs up inside the tube, to then be sent off for testing. Another everyday example is what happens when a paint brush is dipped in paint and the paint "climbs" up between the narrow channels in between the bristles of the brush. Then you pick up the brush and the paint is held there, and it doesn't all simply run back out of the brush. While these are simple examples of these basic principles of physics and fluid dynamics, without them straw wouldn't hold water very well and Picasso would have had a much harder time painting his masterpieces.

Right: Hay can be baled alfalfa or any of dozens of different grasses. Hay is fed to livestock as fodder. It contains all the seed heads inside the bale. Hay is usually green colored, heavy, usually costs a bit more, and is delicious and nutritious for livestock. But hay is less desirable for bale gardens.

Straw is sold in many local garden centers and farm stores in autumn for seasonal decoration, or to use as insulation around certain marginally hardy perennials or shrubs. Look for bales in the fall and put them out in your garden over the winter; this will not hurt them to sit outside until spring when you'll roll them into place to start prepping them for your garden.

Finding your bales: Make friends with a farmer

Finding bales of straw should not be difficult, but the costs will vary based on the buyer's proximity to the source of the bales themselves. Farmer-direct prices will vary based on your region, with some as low as $2 per bale. If you purchase your bales from a secondary market like a garden center or a feed store, your cost could run as high as $6 per bale. Shop around to lower your upfront costs significantly. It may not be worth a drive to the countryside if you only want one or two bales, but if you are looking for ten or twenty bales, then take that drive. One tip is to shop for bales in the fall for next spring's garden, as straw is always more available in the fall.

Farmers would rather sell the bales just after harvest than have to go to all the work of storing them, only to pull them out of storage the next spring. You'll see bales everywhere once you are on the look-out for them. The local church may use them to create their outdoor Nativity scene at Christmas, and another family has them stacked up as insulation around the foundation of their old house. Straw bales are like Volkswagen Beetles: you never notice them until you're looking, then they turn up everywhere.

Straw for growing plants

The "worthless" wet bales of straw, or dry bales for that matter, are perfect for anyone who'd like to grow fresh vegetables, flowers or delicious greens and fruits. Using a bale of straw just like a rectangular planting container, anyone can grow his or her favorite crops, with little effort, no weeding, and minimal bending over. The whole point of this book is to show you how to turn a few bales of straw into an amazing, productive, bountiful garden for growing

ONLINE HELP FOR FINDING BALES (www.strawbalemarket.com)

Many farmers have converted to generating large round bales instead of rectangular ones since the labor involved in baling is minimized with larger bales, and the demand for the smaller square bales has dropped off over the years. It is possible that some farmers would be willing to bale for you in small bales if they knew in advance that they would be able to sell those bales and earn a bigger profit than they do on the larger round bales. This disconnect between supplier and user has been the main reason for starting www.strawbalemarket.com a national/international directory of straw bale suppliers, which puts bale buyers in direct contact with local farmers near them who have straw bales for sale. This allows farmers to make a larger profit margin selling bales to the gardener, while still saving the gardener money by allowing them to source the bales directly cutting out the middle man.

your own food. You won't need special tools, advanced training, horticultural expertise or a big backyard with beautiful productive soil.

You will need three things to guarantee a successful straw bale garden: one or more bales of straw; at least six hours a day of direct sunlight; and water. I will give you the step-by-step instructions, proven to work in any corner of planet earth where you can get access to these three things. The outer shell of the straw bale, which will be tied up tightly with twine, will act as the "container." The inside of the straw bale will begin to decompose quickly so it can provide the necessary nutrients. As you "condition" the bale with additional fertilizer it will become an incredibly productive container garden, ready to plant with about anything you can think of. You'll have a large capacity container, filled with beautiful planting media within about two weeks, and all for a price that would make even my depression era grandma Josephine smile.

Carrying a heavy bale of straw around the yard can be difficult even for a big, brutish man like me. Try using a tarp for a little assistance. Roll the bale onto one end of the tarp, now wet down the grass on the route you plan to take, and you'll see the bale slides easily anywhere you want to go.

Water is essential to a Straw Bale Garden

When a bale of straw gets wet, several things begin to happen. First, the moisture seeps into the bale and helps to feed the naturally occurring bacteria already present there. Once in contact with moisture, the bacteria grow and reproduce, and as part of the natural process the bacteria begin to consume the straw, causing decomposition and decay. Bacteria also thrive on nitrogen, so without a source of nitrogen to feed them, the bacteria will usually grow at a slow rate. Not much nitrogen is present in straw, so the bale will begin to decompose very slowly. If the bale would happen to be lying on the ground, the bacteria in the bale will actually absorb nitrogen from the adjoining soil, fueling growth and accelerating the breakdown of the straw bale. Within a short time, a bale lying on the ground outside will have rotten twine, and any attempt to pick up that waterlogged bale will usually lead to straw everywhere across the farmyard. Leave that bale untouched for about two years and it becomes completely unrecognizable, reduced to a small pile of compost. The remaining compost supports the lush growth of any seed that happens to drop by, and most often in a farmyard it produces a crop of beautiful weeds.

DEER
FENCE

Planning YOUR STRAW BALE GARDEN

A STRAW BALE GARDEN CAN BE established virtually anywhere, as long as the location selected gets full sun and water is accessible. In the SBG world, the soil that you may be "cursed" with in your backyard is irrelevant to your success. I am familiar with several Straw Bale Gardens that have been grown on top of the asphalt in the corner of a parking lot, and the gardens grew beautifully. What's under the bales is completely irrelevant to this method of gardening because the roots establish in the bales, not in the soil. The bales can rest on any surface, including grass, packed gravel, loose pea rock and even solid concrete. If the garden is established on top of contaminated soil, put down a layer of landscape fabric beneath the bales. This will prevent any roots from possibly growing through the bales and into the surface soil and absorbing anything that could be harmful to the plant or to those who eat the crop grown. The soil acts only as a drain for water that runs out of the straw bales and as a mechanism to hold the bales in place.

If the area chosen to set up the Straw Bale Garden has a slight slope, this can be advantageous because it will keep water from pooling underneath the bales and making the aisles between the rows muddy after a heavy rain. As much as possible, avoid any area where water tends to stand after a rainfall. Mud puddles are not fun to stand in while you are tending your garden.

Opposite: This garden was established by the Penn State Cooperative Extension in State College, Pennsylvania—literally in the parking lot. Proof that anyone can grow beautiful crops pretty much anywhere.

HANDLING SLOPE

Straw Bale Gardening on a slope is definitely possible. Position the bales so they run up and down the slope rather than across the hillside. If you turn them sideways the bales can easily tip over, and that could be a disaster if it happened at the wrong time during the season. Use a few wood stakes next to any bales that may be precariously perched on a hillside. It will let you sleep well when the wind blows in the wrong direction, without concern that you'll wake up to a horizontal garden disaster.

Plant it where the sun shines

It is vital that the site selected for the garden has full sun exposure, with a minimum of six to eight hours of sunlight each day. Less than full sun will limit the vegetable crops that will grow well, and will prevent other crops from achieving maximum yield. Limiting sunlight not only reduces photosynthetic activity, slowing plant development and ripening, but it also slows the drying of morning dew from the leaves of your crops. Wet leaves spread disease! If a leaf has even a speck of fungus, mold, virus or bacteria present on the leaf, the diseased leaf can act like a petri dish and in a humid environment the surface can rapidly reproduce and spread that disease.

Care should be taken to keep leaf surfaces as dry as possible for good overall plant health and better crop production. If possible, pick a location that allows for morning sun exposure so that leaves dry early in the day. Halting the spread of fungus, mold, virus or bacterial infections on plant leaves can be as simple as keeping the leaves dry. Make it your practice to prune off any diseased leaves whenever you see them. This will help limit the spread of problems to other plants.

Place your garden so it gets good morning light and you'll spend less time removing diseased leaves.

Productivity vs. creativity

The most productive and efficient garden will have single file rows of bales positioned end to end. This allows easy access to the plants on the surface from either side of the row, and maximizes the air circulation around plants and leaf surfaces exposed to direct sunlight. If space is limited it is possible to run two rows side by side. This way, bales will still be accessible from the outside. Some people like to line up their bales in a variety of creative ways, making squares or boxes around squares, or zigzag bales to make a really funky design. This will work okay, but I do not recommended putting any more than two rows side by side. Always allow for a minimum four feet of space between each row of bales. More than four feet is best if you have the space available and can use it to stretch out the distance between rows. Four feet will allow a wheelbarrow or garden wagon to move easily up and down between the rows.

Say "No!" to overhead sprinklers and "Yes!" to a humble soaker hose.

Stop the insanity! Turn off your sprinklers and turn on a soaker hose

Using overhead sprinklers in any vegetable garden is poor cultural practice and should be avoided in a vegetable garden if possible. The droplets of water being sprayed under pressure can land on a diseased or infected leaf surface up to 40 feet away and mechanically distribute that infection to dozens of surrounding leaves with a giant splash. Invest in a few soaker hoses and the disease problems in the Straw Bale Garden or any garden for that matter will disappear, or at least be reduced dramatically. Your water bills will also shrink, as water will now be applied directly to the roots and not everywhere else. Those flying drops also evaporate at a much higher rate than water applied directly to the root zone. Hand watering is still effective, just use a watering wand so water can be applied under the leaves and avoid getting them wet every time the garden is watered. Remember, wet leaves spread disease!

Accessibility and Straw Bale Gardens

For those many gardeners who use wheelchairs, you'll find that Straw Bale Gardening works very well for you. Keep your rows of bales 4 feet apart and put down some ½ inch or thicker plywood between the rows. The plywood will keep the weeds from growing and make it easy to roll and turn in between the rows. Plan to replace the plywood every few years, because it will decompose quickly when lying on top of the soil and since it is being constantly soaked with water. The raised height of the bales makes it much easier for someone in a wheelchair to plant and harvest, and it is much less expensive than building raised beds.

MY GRANDMA ALWAYS SAID, "Watering the garden is the most fun I have all day." She would water every day by hand, inspecting leaves as she watered each plant and removing any leaves that showed signs of infection, and always looking for insects and removing as many harmful ones she found by hand. If any problem poked its head up in the garden, she was on top of it right away, and this was because she watered (inspected) her garden daily. This slow walk through the garden gave her time to thoroughly inspect every plant almost every day. This isn't something I do, to be honest. Once my soaker hoses are in place, you won't see me dragging hoses around my vegetable garden much during the season. All of my watering is done automatically via timers that go off while I am still asleep early in the morning. Like most people these days, I don't have the time to water my garden by hand every day. Sorry Grandma!

Laying the garden out in straight rows with 4 to 6 feet between the rows is the most efficient and productive plan. Others might choose to be creative with their garden layout, and that works okay as well, but it does make the wire trellis more difficult to build over the bales.

Crowding plants together on top of bales that are already spaced too closely together can be detrimental. This crowding limits air circulation and sun exposure to the plants. If multiple bales are crowded together, it quickly becomes more difficult to reach the inside bales. If you have to lean over one or two bales to plant and harvest on an adjoining bale, the job becomes more difficult. Being creative in designing your garden can be just as much fun as trying a new method for gardening like Straw Bale Gardening. So be creative if you like, and make whatever shapes you feel look good. You will have to figure out how to support any climbing plants above the bales, so do keep this in mind as you create your own designs. You'll see that the trellis system we show you how to build later in the book works best if the bales are in a single straight row. But this certainly isn't the only way to set up your Straw Bale Garden, and the straight trellis isn't the only way to support climbing plants either.

"Before I had my knee replaced last June I planted a veggie Straw Bale Garden. It's made it so easy for me to maintain because I don't have to bend down. I'm really looking forward to this year's garden since I can walk well now. So glad I found SBG. Thanks Joel!" Susan

Using some ground cover, such as wood mulch (shown), between the rows of bales is the easiest and cheapest way to keep weeds or grass from growing up between the rows. If your plan is to grow vining plants like squash, watermelon or pumpkins, those vines will grow everywhere, so you must keep the grass and weeds from competing with the vines in those areas between the rows.

Landscape fabric (shown), newspaper, cardboard, old carpeting, wood mulch or a thick layer of loose straw can all be used to prevent grass and weeds from growing between the rows of bales you have set up.

Cover up trouble between rows of bales

It is possible to simply mow the grass or weeds that grow up in between the rows of bales, in order to maintain a neat-looking garden. However, if crops that produce prolific vines such as squash, pumpkin or watermelon are started in the bales, the vines will quickly grow everywhere around the bale and cover the grass or weeds that surround the bales. Training some of these vines up onto the wire trellis above the bales works well, but the fruit production will be concentrated on the vines that are allowed to grow and develop on the ground beside the bales. The exceptions here are cucumbers, tomatoes and some other vines with smaller fruits; keep these vines completely trained up and growing on the wire trellis. Conversely, trying to grow a 20-pound watermelon or giant pumpkin on the wire trellis is virtually impossible, so allow those vines to spread onto the ground around the bales. If left uncovered, the grass or weeds in between the rows of bales will end up growing above the vines and shading them, causing decline and significantly less productivity. The squash, pumpkins or watermelons that develop on top of grass and weeds between the rows would lie in contact with the damp grass and would be more likely to mold or rot. This problem can be avoided by putting down a weed barrier in between the rows of bales. Fruits lying on top of the weed barrier will dry quickly and never have to compete for light with weeds or grass.

A layer of landscape fabric works very well to prevent vegetation growth from below. Many materials can be used to prevent vegetation growth between rows of bales, including everything from old carpeting, cardboard boxes, several layers of newspaper, a deep layer of loose straw or wood mulch. Essentially any barrier can be put down to prevent sunlight from penetrating down to the soil so seeds will not germinate or grow plants from below.

TAKE A PASS ON PLASTIC

Do not put down sheet plastic, PVC tarps or any kind of impermeable layer, as it will keep moisture from soaking into the ground. This, in turn, raises the humidity level in the garden. High humidity is not good for a garden because it encourages the growth, development and spread of disease. Any impermeable surface may also grow algae, making it slippery and stinky! The temptation to use a tarp or poly sheeting between the rows can be compelling, but you must resist it. It seems like it would work well, but it doesn't—take it from someone who has tried it.

If the vines get out of hand and grow into areas that you have not covered with weed fabric, it works well to slide an asphalt shingle or a piece of wood under each developing melon or pumpkin, and turn the pumpkins upright so the vine stem is facing upward. This keeps the fruits from rotting and helps them develop the pleasing shape that we're accustomed to.

I actually live in "the Gopher state." How about you?

Minnesota, where I live, is known as "the Gopher state," and the name fits: even our University mascot is Goldy the Gopher. We have several kinds of gophers here, but no matter where you live rodents can be a real problem in a vegetable garden. If you live in a part of the world where gophers are a potential problem, I can tell you it is much easier to prevent problems than to try to get rid of them once they are entrenched. Unroll either chicken wire or hardware cloth (it is not cloth, it is wire mesh—they just call it hardware cloth, and I don't know why) onto the ground before putting down your bales. Gophers and other burrowing rodents like to dig in from under the bales. With this simple wire barrier down, the problem is easily prevented. If you don't put down the wire, and the gophers move in, this option is off the table, since there is no way to lift the bales once they are waterlogged and beginning to decompose. At the end of the season you'll discover an added bonus: The wire actually works well as a kind of toboggan to drag your decomposed bales over to the compost pile.

Set up the bales so the strings that bind the bales together are located on the sides, and not on top. There are several reasons to do this. The main one is simply to keep the strings out of the way when you plant the surface. If you cut a string accidentally, fix it as quickly as you can. The strings are part of the "container" and without the strings the compression inside the bale is lost. That higher compression is part of the reason the bales decompose quickly (that is a good thing).

Cut side up

Take notice that straw bales have two distinctly different sides. One is the cut side and it looks as if the ends of the straws are aligned and have been sliced off with a knife. The other side of the bale is the folded side and appears as if the straw stems have been folded over in the baling process. It is ideal to orient the bales so they have the cut side positioned up, because this allows much easier penetration of water and granular fertilizer into the bale during the conditioning process. If you end up with the folded side of the bale facing up, it will still work fine, but may take a bit more time and effort to work the fertilizer and water down into the interior of the bales.

Every bale will have a cut side (prickly side) and a folded side. For gardening, orient the bales so the cut side of the bale is facing up. It will be easier to get the fertilizer and water to work down into the bale from the cut side.

Strings on the sides

The strings of the straw bales should be around the sides of the bale and not on the top and bottom surfaces of the bales. If the strings happen to be running on the cut side of the bale, ignore the cut side and keep the strings to the side. It will be a bit more work to get the fertilizer worked down into the bale, but keeping the strings on the side of the bale will serve another purpose later on as well. Keeping the strings to the side is also important to avoid damage to the strings during planting, which would destroy the "container." A sharp hand spade digging a shallow hole in the top of the bale can easily slice a string, releasing the compression that exists inside the bale and is essential to its quick decomposition. Keep the strings intact at all costs, and if one is ever accidentally cut, do your best to retie a new string around the bale quickly. Bales of straw are like Humpty Dumpty: If they break open you'll never get them put back together again. If one breaks open, I suggest you put that bale into your compost pile and start over. You may find other uses for loose straw around the garden, but loose straw will not work for Straw Bale Gardening.

NYLON STRING

In the distant past farmers used baling wire instead of baling twine. Today some farmers are still using hemp twine, which is a strong natural fiber, but will, of course, decompose like any other organic material if the right conditions exist. Nylon string has become very common for binding bales these days. The good, and the bad, thing about nylon string is that is doesn't decompose, EVER. If a string falls off of a bale in a farmer's field, a farmer 1,000 years from now will still be dealing with that same string. There are no worries with nylon however, because even if a bale has been sitting around for a while the strings will never break.

Tools and Materials

STRAW BALES

Look for big and heavy bales. This means they are tightly compressed and will not shrink too much during the growing season. I recommend five bales of production per individual in the family, so a twenty-bale garden will keep a family of four in produce for the season. Make sure you are getting "harvested" straw bales. In rare circumstances the straw gets cut and baled without having the seed heads harvested, which means the entire bale would sprout and grow "hair" and you would have a Chia Pet growing in your garden. Make sure it is straw and not hay, as discussed earlier. Generally, in most of the world hay is more of a commodity than straw, thus it usually costs more per bale.

A dry bale of straw can weigh anywhere from 35 to75 pounds depending on how big it is, and that is only determined by the farmer and how he has set up his baler. Bales can also differ in density, as the farmer can adjust how tightly the straw is squeezed as the bales are created. Look for big, heavy, dense bales, as they hold up better during the long gardening season. Usually the price is per bale, so get the most straw you can for the price.

Just about any inexpensive lawn fertilizer (most brands found at any store) will work to condition your bales. Lawn fertilizers typically have a high nitrogen content and are very soluble. Use caution, however, to stay away from anything with herbicide (weed killer) mixed in. You don't want to apply any herbicides where you intend to grow plants.

FERTILIZER

Inexpensive lawn fertilizer from any local garden center or hardware store will work for conditioning your bales. You will need approximately one pound for each bale you plan to plant, so five pounds will suffice for five bales. The three numbers on the side of every bag of fertilizer are its content analysis. 29-0-4 would be 29% nitrogen (N), 0% phosphorous (P) and 4% potassium (K). All fertilizer bags will have the same percentage analysis provided in the same order: N-P-K. Look for a lawn fertilizer with at least 20% nitrogen, as it will ensure that the bacteria in the bales are activated quickly. Make certain the nitrogen in the fertilizer selected is NOT a slow-release type. Many combinations of fertilizers exist, but do not use anything with herbicide, weed killer or crabgrass preventer.

Organic fertilizer is easy to find in stores these days. Make sure to read the content analysis to see how much actual nitrogen, phosphorus and potassium is contained in the brand you are considering. Higher percentages typically mean you are getting more for your money, so shop around.

Wood ash can be used to provide potassium, but it needs to be blended with other ingredients.

If you are an organic gardener, you'll need approximately three pounds of Milorganite®, blood meal, feather meal or similar organic source of fertilizer with at least 5% nitrogen, for each bale. For example, buy 15 pounds of organic fertilizer to condition five bales of straw. You'll notice that the organic fertilizers will usually have a much lower percentage of nitrogen, and often little or no phosphorus or potassium. Obviously this is the reason we will need to use more volume of the organic versus the refined fertilizer.

A small bag of garden fertilizer that contains some phosphorus and potassium (the second two numbers in the analysis on every bag) will also be needed. Look for a 10-10-10—it is a common garden fertilizer sold almost everywhere. If you want to stay with organic fertilizers, look for bone meal or fish meal, which are good sources for phosphorus. Wood ashes or kelp meal are great organic sources of potassium. Mix half wood ashes together with another phosphorus source to make a balanced organic fertilizer and this concoction will provide all the remaining essential nutrients plants need as they get started growing.

STEEL "T" POSTS

A visit to a farm supply store or a building center will help you find 7- or 8-foot-tall steel fence posts. The "T"-style posts are the best. They will last a lifetime, so it is a one-time investment. They usually cost around $5 to $7 each for the tall ones, and you should buy the tallest posts they have available. The "T" is a reference to the shape of the shank of the post, if you were to look at it from above. These posts often have a stabilization flange welded near the bottom, which serves to keep the post from wiggling loose once it is pounded in place.

Named for their profile, "T" posts work well to support the wire trellis you'll want to erect above your bales.

POST POUNDER

This is a special tool that slides over the top of the post like a giant cap on an ink pen. The pounder is weighted to help with the force needed to pound through hard soil. The handles serve as a place to grab ahold and by raising it up and smacking it down, the post is quickly pounded into the soil to the proper depth. Without this tool you'll be trying to hit the end of that post with a hammer and you'll surely miss and hurt yourself or someone you love. Rent one from the local rental center, or buy one for you and all your neighbors to use. Because once they see your garden you'll have lots of new straw bale gardeners in your neighborhood, so they will need to borrow your post pounder for their own posts next year.

A post pounder is a tool that you won't use often, but it is nearly impossible to get your posts in straight, and safely, without one. Rental stores often have them available.

2 X 4 DIMENSIONAL LUMBER

You'll want to stretch a 2 x 4 between the posts at the top. This serves to hold the posts apart when the wires are pulled tight between the posts. Without the board across the top between the posts, the wires pull the posts over and they get loose and tend to sag down in the middle. If the span of your row is more than 12 feet, you'll be better off with a 2 x 6 instead, because the 2 x 4 will sag in the middle. Dimensional lumber longer than 20 feet can be difficult to find and haul, so 5 bales each 4 feet long may be the longest span you'll want to stretch between posts.

14-GAUGE ELECTRIC FENCING WIRE

Buy enough wire to stretch a distance equal to eight full lengths of your straw bales if you were to set them up in a row. Stick with 14-gauge wire, anything lighter and you risk snapping the wire under the weight of your vines. Heavier wire can be difficult to manipulate with bare hands, but if you are up to it, try some 12-gauge wire, and you'll surely never need to replace a wire for any reason.

Fourteen-gauge electric fencing wire works best to create the wire trellis above the bales. Heavier gauge wire can be hard to cut and difficult to bend by hand. Wear leather gloves: There is nothing worse than starting out the gardening season with a cut on your hand!

Soaker hoses work well to get even, gentle water distribution over your bales. Keeping the water off the leaves is one key to controlling the spread of disease in any vegetable garden, and a soaker-style hose is the perfect solution.

SOAKER HOSE

Acquire enough soaker hose to stretch the full length of your bales when lined up in a single row. I like the seeping style of hose, because it lets water leak out through the walls of the hose. You may be familiar with the flat PVC "pin prick" style of hose. These are popular for watering a long narrow area like a boulevard strip of lawn. This style of hose works also, you'll simply turn it upside down so the tiny holes face down into the bale, rather than spraying up in all directions.

HEAVY DUTY GARDEN HOSE

Buy a heavy duty hose long enough to stretch from the spigot you'll be using over to the garden, where you'll connect up to the soaker hose. Look for a 100% rubber, reinforced garden hose, avoiding vinyl hoses. Good hoses will have solid cast connector fittings. The couplers will not bend out of round if stepped on or driven over. A good hose will be more expensive but will last a very long time; like so many things, cheaper isn't always less expensive in the long run.

Buy a heavy duty garden hose, since the cheaper ones will not last for long when used regularly.

WORK SMARTER NOT HARDER!

I like to make a shallow slit in the grass from my faucet over to the garden's edge, with a flat spade. I tuck the garden hose into the slit and step the grass back down over the hose. This "buried" hose is now out of the way for the whole summer. If you are responsible for cutting the lawn at your house, you'll appreciate not having to stop and move that pesky garden hose out of the way every time you cut the grass during the year.

HOSE END TIMER

Loaded with a 9-volt battery, this tool will save you the work of watering your garden every day, as it can be set to turn on any day of the week at any time, for any length of time. Remember that because they drain so well it is impossible to overwater a Straw Bale Garden, so don't worry if it rains in addition to the water you are giving it. To keep from wasting water, you can always override the automatic timer and skip the watering for a day or two when it does rain.

A hose end timer can be set to turn on the flow of water on specific days of the week, for a specified duration, and can be easily adjusted if weather requires an increase or decrease in watering for the garden. If you can set an alarm clock, the hose end timer will be no problem. Most are very simple to operate. They have a battery that easily lasts for an entire season.

HAND TROWEL

This is the only gardening tool you'll need to plant, maintain and harvest the crops in your Straw Bale Garden. Many different sizes and shapes are available. I like the old metal one I have. I like to file down one edge to make it sharp so it doubles as a knife blade if I need to cut something.

Leave your rototiller, rake, shovel and hoe in the garden shed this year. Oil them up well, so they don't rust from nonuse. The only tool you'll need this year is a simple hand trowel.

LANDSCAPE FABRIC

Look for the heavy duty landscape fabric because it does a much better job and will last for several seasons. The less expensive landscape fabric will tear more easily during installation and from foot traffic. Cover any landscape fabric with clean wood mulch, straw or something to prevent the sun's UV rays from breaking down the fabric. It will need to be replaced every few years, because weed seeds will accumulate on top of the fabric and sprout from not only the top of the fabric but also from under the wood mulch or straw. Most manufacturers will also sell plastic "pins" that puncture the fabric to keep it in place for installation, or you can use a few lengths of wire bent in half like giant staples to do the same job. You might choose some other material instead of the landscape fabric to put down between the rows of bales in your garden. Other options might include a thick 8- to 10-inch layer of loose straw, six layers of newspaper, old cardboard boxes, carpeting, wood planks or 4 inches of wood mulch. Anything that can prevent light from penetrating and germinating weed seeds or allowing them to get light to grow up from the soil underneath will work.

Landscape fabric is essentially a woven or perforated synthetic fabric like nylon. The fabric prevents weeds by blocking the light from getting to the seeds and plants in the soil below.

Sterile planting mix will be needed for creating a seedbed and healing in transplants on the surface of the bales. Any sterile mix without weed seeds and without actual soil will work fine.

PLANTING MIX

You will need approximately one cubic foot of "planting mix" for every two bales you plant. This mix must be sterile, without weed seeds or actual soil in it. This is to avoid soil borne disease or other soil borne problems. I like the Miracle Gro® brand and they offer both traditional and 100% organic mixes. They are consistently clean and have slow-release fertilizer mixed in with the mix. One big bag (2 cu. ft.) will suffice for four bales of straw, and any leftover mix can be kept until the following season without any problems.

POLYETHYLENE PLASTIC SHEETING

Available in any home center, hardware store or discount store, you will need a roll of 2- to 3-mil thick, polyethylene plastic sheeting that's 5-feet wide and long enough to easily cover the entire length of your row of bales. Thicker is not better; it can be difficult to work with, and thinner than 2-mil will tear easily and not provide the insulating ability we need. You will find a large assortment of thickness and sizes available, so shop around. It is very easy to cut the sheeting to size with a utility knife, so if you end up with a 10-foot wide roll it can be easily cut in half to make two sheets.

You'll need polyethylene plastic that is 2 to 3 mil thick (do not confuse "mil" with "millimeter") and long enough to cover the length of a row of bales.

Laying Out the Garden

POUND POSTS AT THE END OF EACH ROW

Pound a seven-foot tall or taller steel fence post (T post) at the end of each row of bales. The posts allow a series of wires to be stretched tightly back and forth between the posts above the bales. These posts will run about $5 to $7 at most home centers or farm supply stores. Use a post pounder to drive the post into the ground—it is really the only tool for the job. You can usually rent one from a local tool rental center, or for $15 you can buy one, and keep it for all the new Straw Bale Gardens that will blossom in your neighborhood once the neighbors have spotted your garden.

Using a post pounder, pound the posts in so the stabilizer flange on the bottom of the post is flush with the ground. Make sure the bumpy side of the "T" post is facing away from the row of bales. Double-check as you begin to make sure that you are pounding the posts in plumb (straight up and down).

A length of 2 x 4 lumber mounted between the posts helps to keep the posts from bending over as the wires running between the posts are tightened.

REINFORCE THE POSTS

Mount a length of wood between the posts to keep them pushed apart as you tighten the wires between the posts. A length of 2 x 4 works well for any row of bales up to about 12 feet; however, longer rows require a 2 x 6 because a longer 2 x 4 will really droop in the middle by mid-summer.

Cut a notch in each end of the 2 x 4 wide enough so that the notch will slide over the tongue of the "T" post. Drill a hole through each board near the end to use a short length of wire when hanging the board between the posts. Once the post-to-post wires are tightened up, they will pinch the board between the posts, and hold it in position tightly. The board may start to sag in the middle and need to be replaced every three or four seasons.

Stretch a pair of wires between the posts at 10 inches above the bale, and another pair of wires at 20 inches, then one wire every 10 inches up the post.

PULL WIRES BETWEEN THE POSTS

Run a pair of wires between the posts at 10 inches above the bales and another pair of wires at 20 inches above the bales, and then simply stretch individual wires every ten inches the rest of the way up the posts. These wires will serve a number of purposes throughout the season and are permanent structures that can be left in place for future years of gardening. These wires will create a solid trellis to support vines or to help support other heavy vegetable crops. Without these support wires, it may be necessary to individually stake any plants that require support. When staking a plant individually, the stakes will go all the way through the bale and into the soil for stability. Creating the wire trellis above the bales is easier and more efficient than individual stakes. These wires will also serve as a support for the Straw Bale "Greenhouse." More information about this will come in the Straw Bale Greenhouse chapter

Use north-to-south rows

Setting up the rows of your garden in a north-to-south orientation is recommended. Setting up the garden to capture the first sunlight of the morning helps dry leaves of the dew they often accumulate during the overnight hours. Remember that wet leaves spread disease, so getting the rising suns warmth on the leaves early is helpful. The prevailing westerly winds that blow our way all summer will hit the bales broadside and work up and around the plants in the top of the bale. This airflow and circulation helps keep the leaves dry and thus, healthy. A bit of wind circulating around a plant can help discourage insects as well. A bug is usually looking to either eat lunch or lay eggs on a leaf. Most bugs would rather not bother with a leaf that is being jostled around by a little breeze but instead would prefer to jump over to a leaf that is lower to the ground, still, shady, and undisturbed. This constant movement from the wind also helps plants build stem taper, thickness and strength. I call this "dancing" when the plants move back and forth in the wind, and I find that dancing is good for both people and plants. Any garden that is planted in an area that gets no wind flow is bound to be plagued with disease and insect problems, and will probably have many weak-stemmed plants that snap easily once the heavy fruits begin to develop later in the season. Establish your garden away from buildings or fences to allow as much wind flow as possible. Contrary to most teachings it doesn't hurt the garden at all. As long as you keep the garden watered well and enough moisture is present in the root zone the wind will actually benefit your garden.

Opposite: As the vines and plants grow up the trellis wires, they will grow more evenly if the rows run north to south. The morning sun will fall on one side of the wire trellis and the afternoon sun will fall on the other side. Note how evenly the vines have developed on the wire trellis pictured here.

GET OFF THE MERRY-GO-ROUND

Many vegetable gardening books spend a great deal of time addressing proper crop rotation of vegetables. No rotation of crops is needed with Straw Bale Gardening. In addition, the idea in traditional soil gardening is that certain pests that are soil borne, including insects, viruses and fungi, are discouraged by rotation because they attack one variety of vegetable but not another. Since we are not using the soil at all when Straw Bale Gardening and instead are making brand new compost each year inside the fresh bale, we don't need to consider any of these issues. No crop rotation is needed.

A strip of shiny metallic tape works well to keep the birds from sitting on the wires above your lettuce crop and leaving behind their own brand of fertilizer.

Tip

Tie some short lengths of "bird tape" to a few posts in your Straw Bale Garden, birds hate it, and they will likely stay away from your garden. I have used many varieties, but Irri-Tape™ seems to work best in my experience. It is available from many places online.

Keep the vines on the trellis balanced

As plants climb up the wire trellis above the bales, having sun on both sides of the trellis throughout the day keeps the vegetation balanced on both sides of the trellis. With a row running north to south, the morning sun hits the vines that have grown up the trellis on the east side in the morning and on the west side in the afternoon, keeping the growth balanced. If the bales are oriented east and west, then the south side of the trellis would get sunshine all day, while the north side gets little exposure. The south side of the trellis has vines flourishing while the north side declines, and this causes an imbalance in growth on the trellis and is less efficient and productive.

Opposite page: With your bales laid out in a logical fashion, your posts firmly in place and your wire trellis tightly strung, you are now ready to begin the process of conditioning your bales.

Irritate the birds

Nobody wants to have birds leaving their own brand of bird fertilizer on the leaves or fruits of plants that you are planning to harvest within a few days. If birds are leaving their "mark" in your garden, try scaring them off by tying a length of bird tape on the posts in your Straw Bale Garden. The sparkling sun reflection and the crinkling sound can be very effective in keeping birds from perching on the wire trellis. The brand called Irri-Tape® Bird Repellant Tape seems to work very well, but others can also be used if you find them to be effective. I am not certain why the birds avoid it, and none of the birds I've asked have been willing to comment I just know it works.

SINGLE-BALE GARDEN with tomato cage

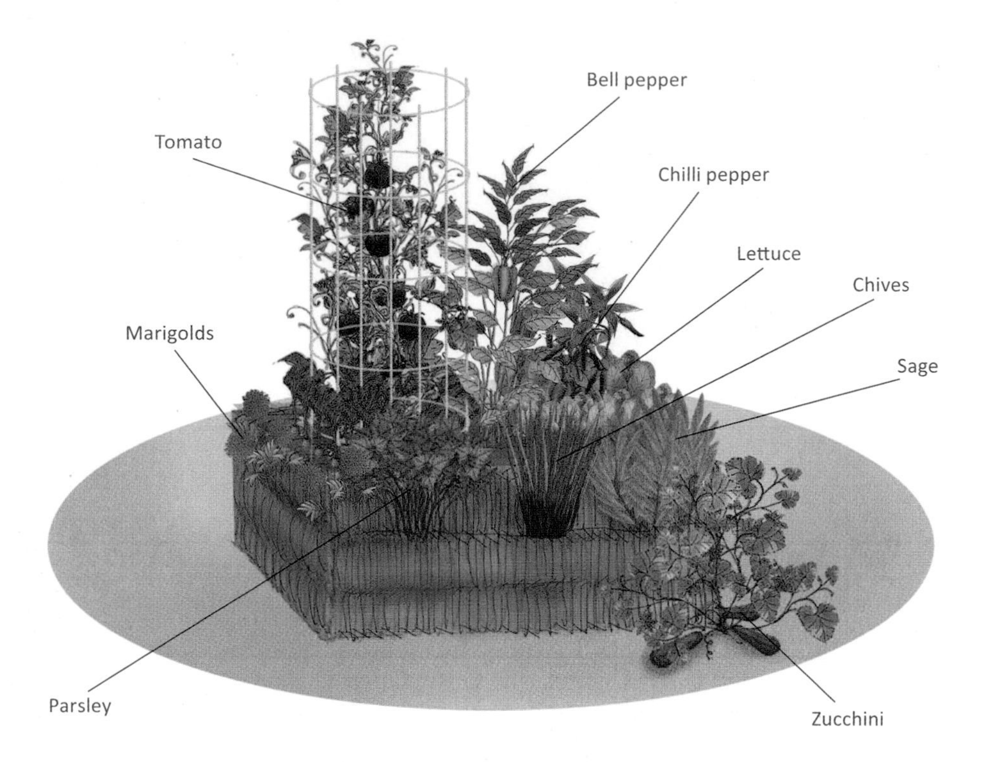

SINGLE-BALE GARDEN with fan trellis

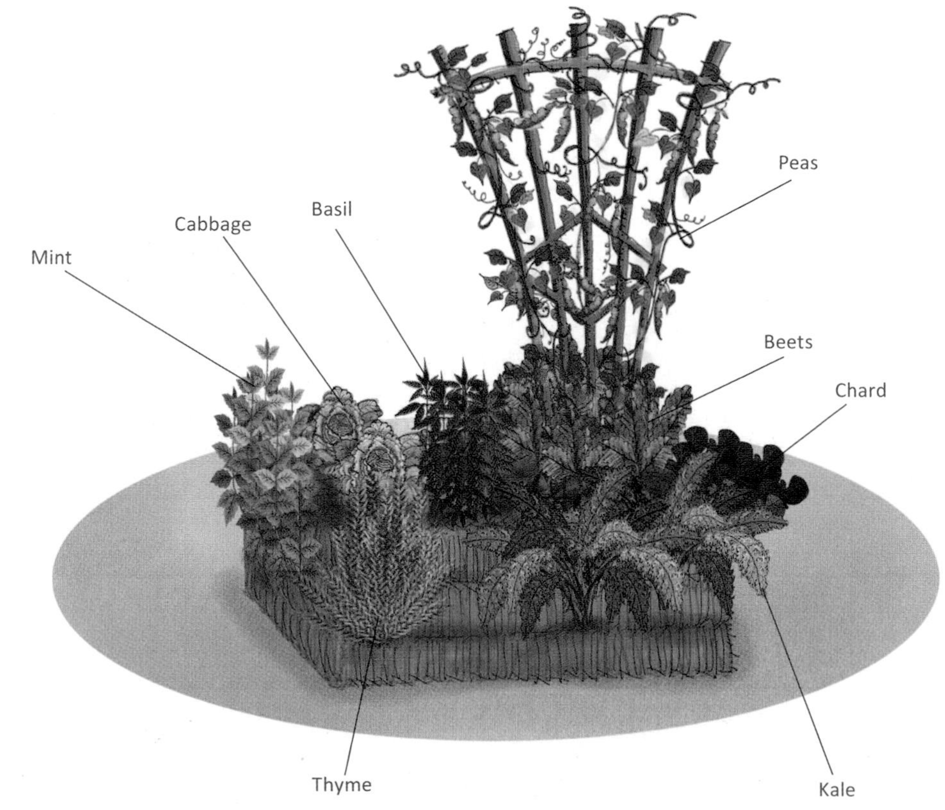

TWO-BALE GARDEN with wood trellis

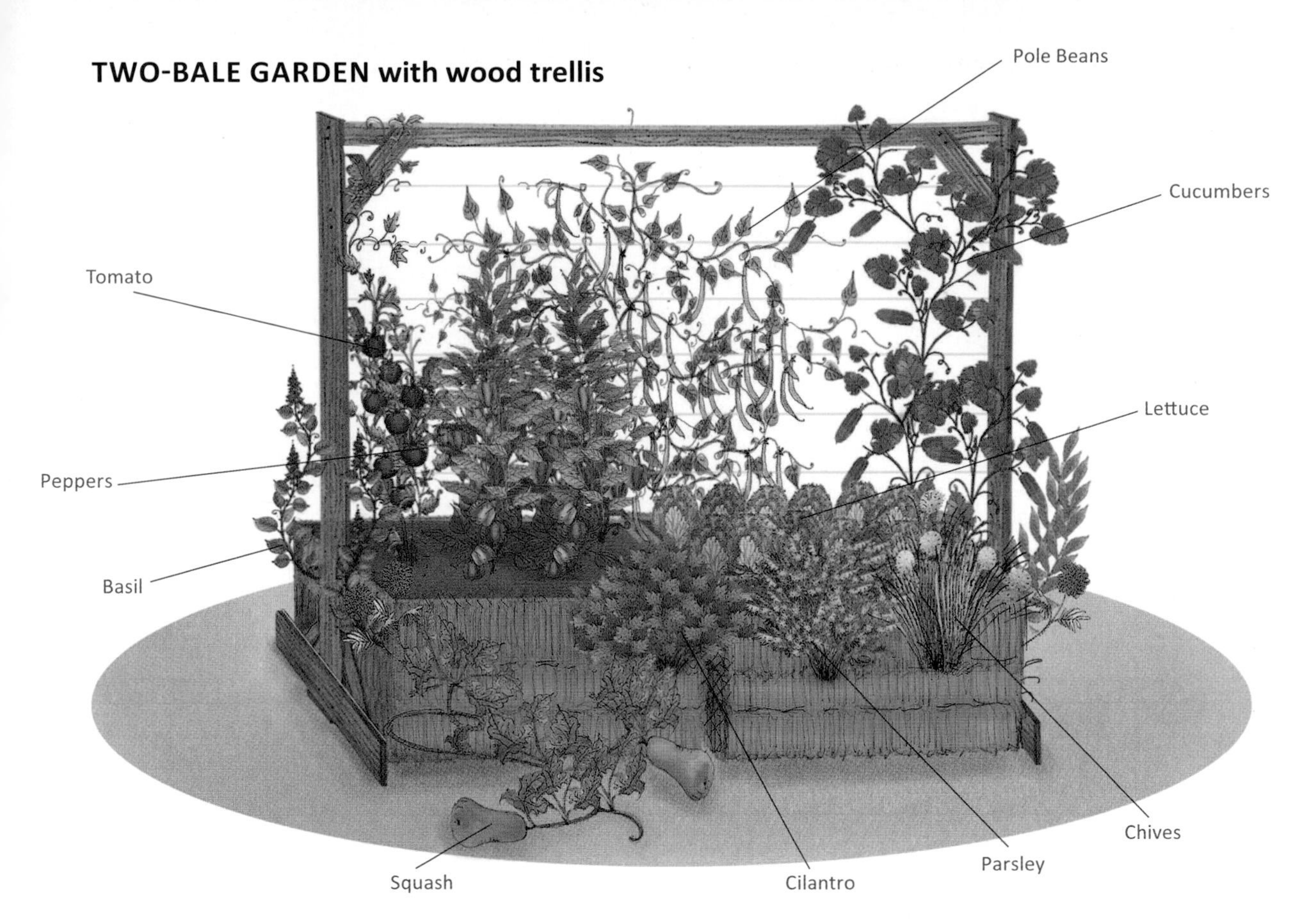

TWO-BALE GARDEN with PVC trellis

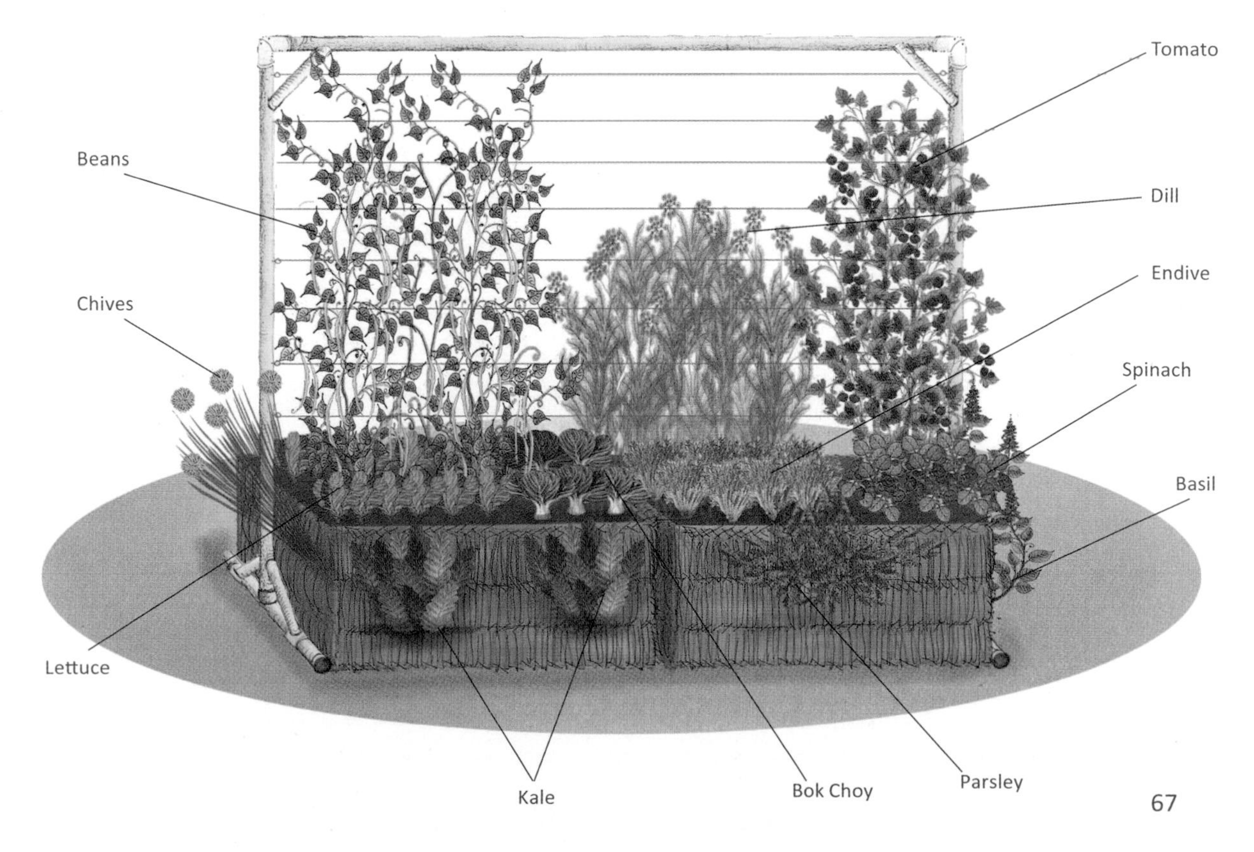

THREE-BALE GARDEN: Layout and Suggested Plants

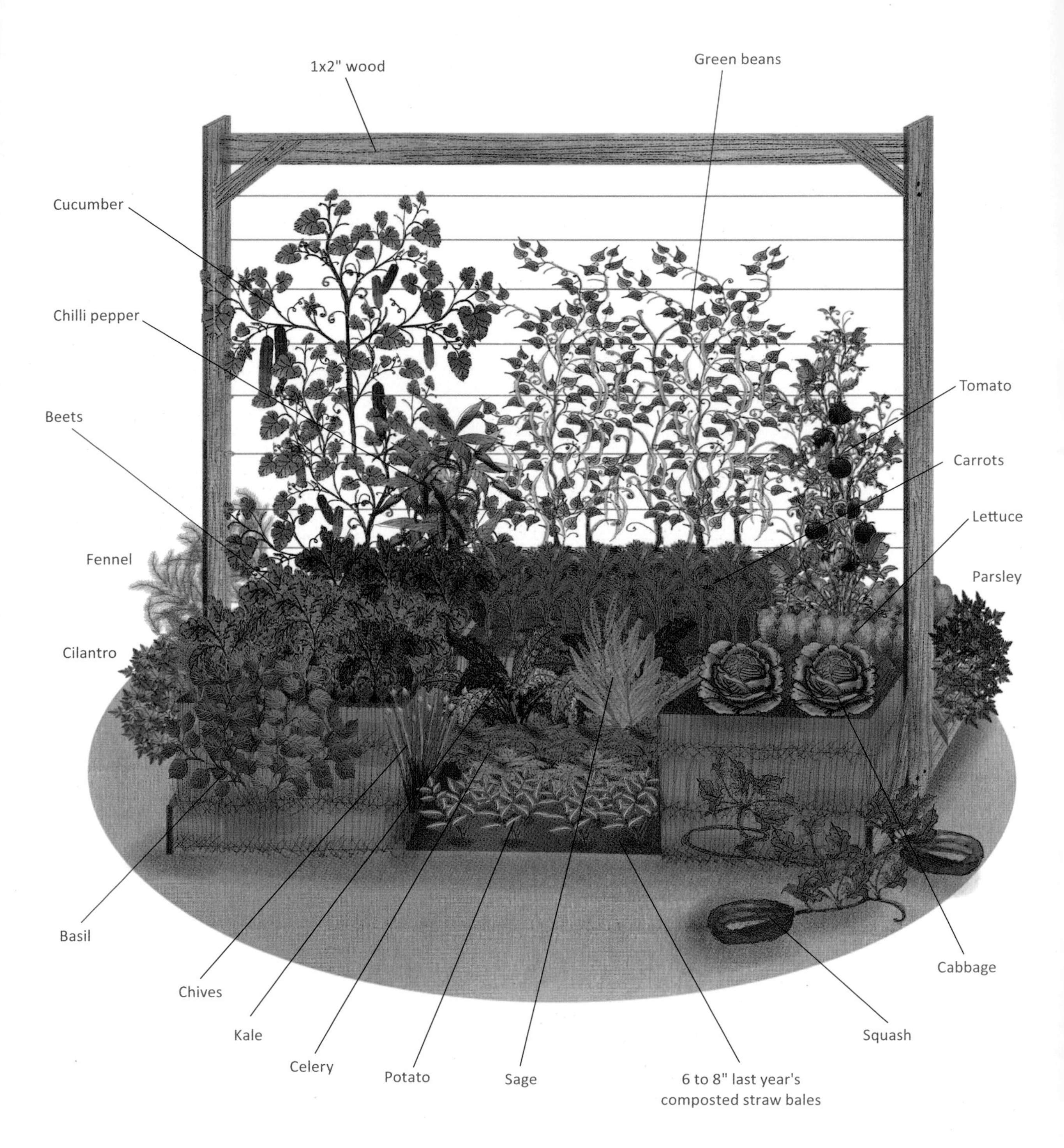

FIVE-BALE GARDEN: Layout and Suggested Plants

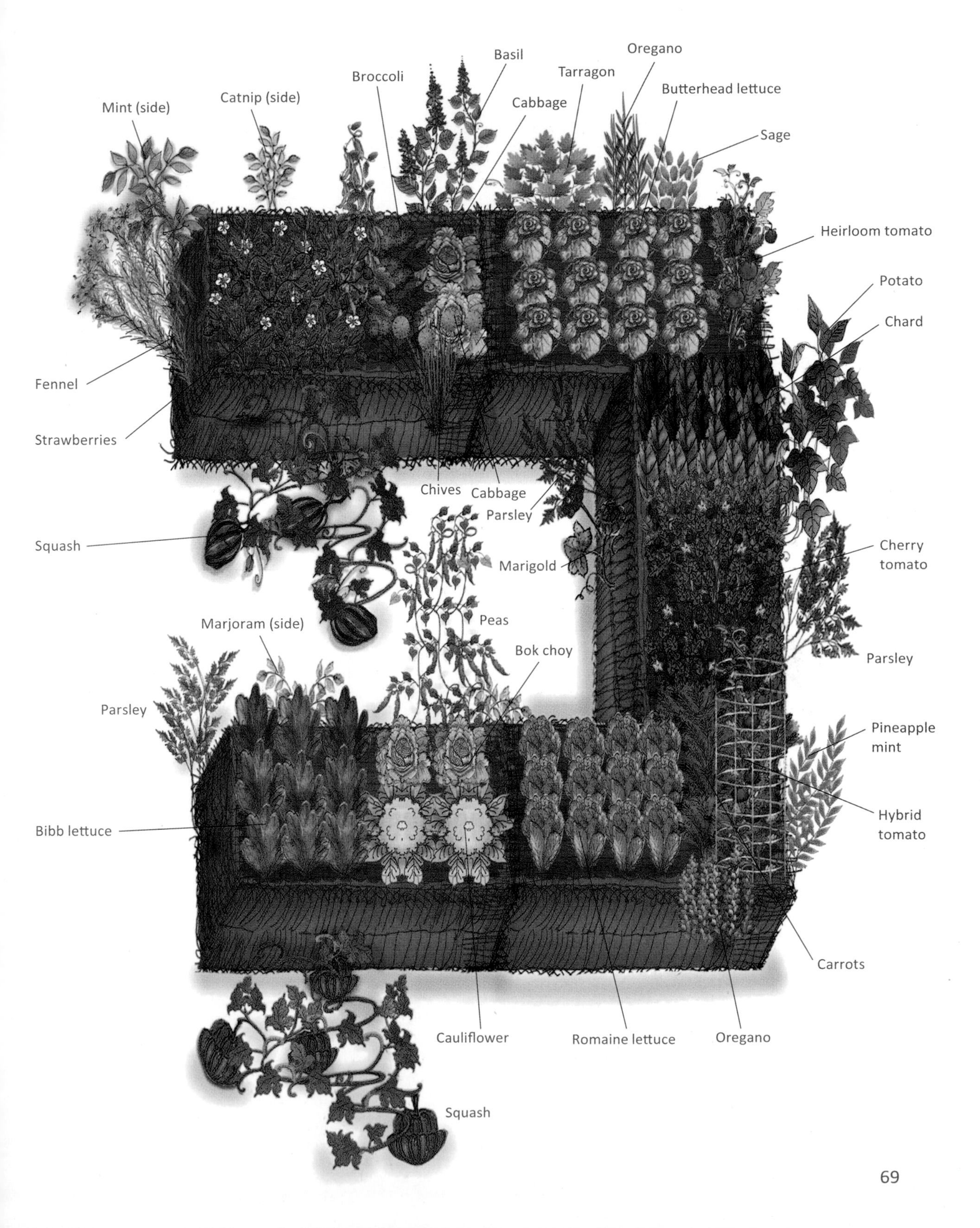

TEN-BALE GARDEN: Layout and Suggested Plants

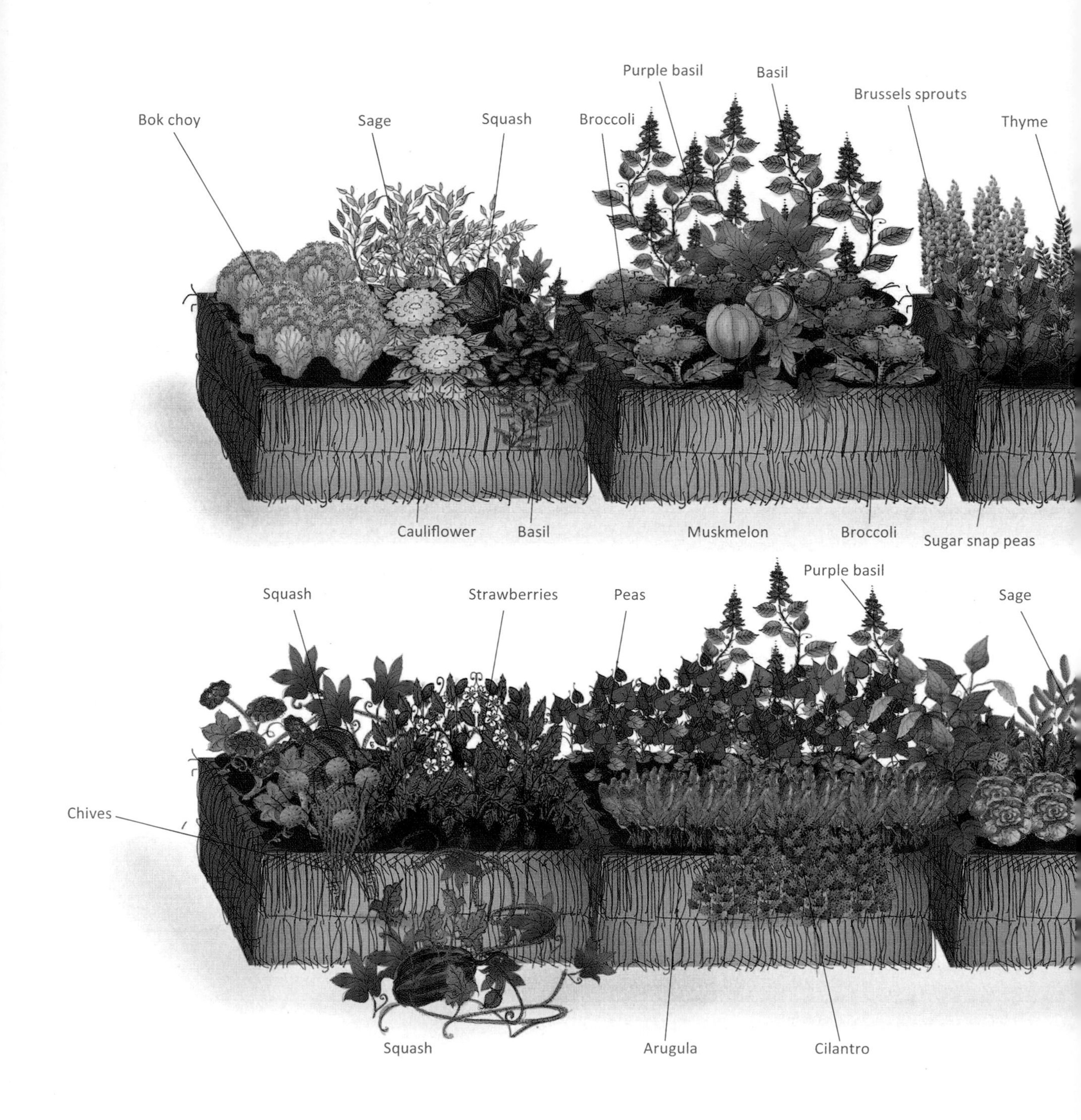

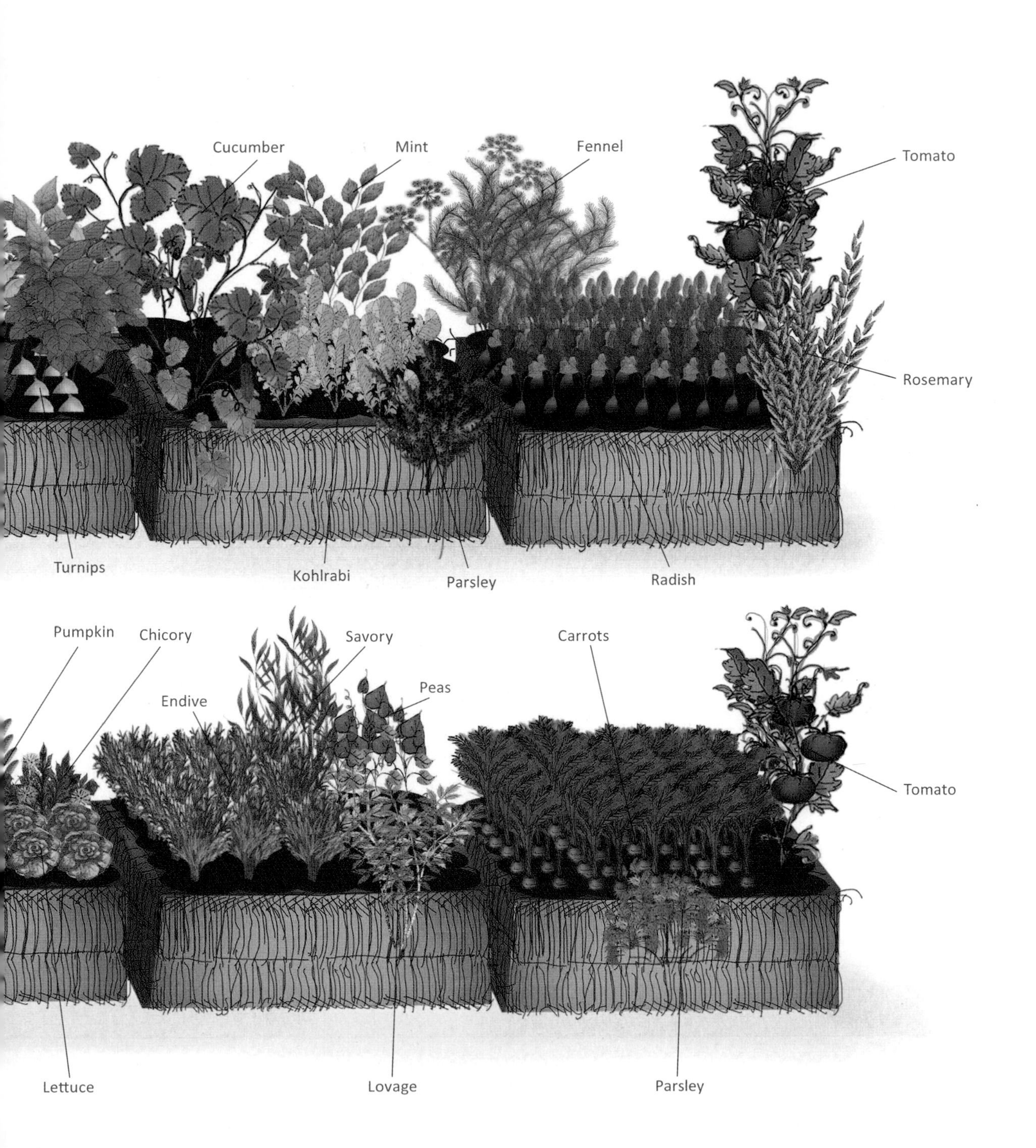
Cucumber
Mint
Fennel
Tomato
Rosemary
Turnips
Kohlrabi
Parsley
Radish
Pumpkin
Chicory
Savory
Carrots
Endive
Peas
Tomato
Lettuce
Lovage
Parsley

FIFTEEN-BALE GARDEN: Layout and Suggested Plants

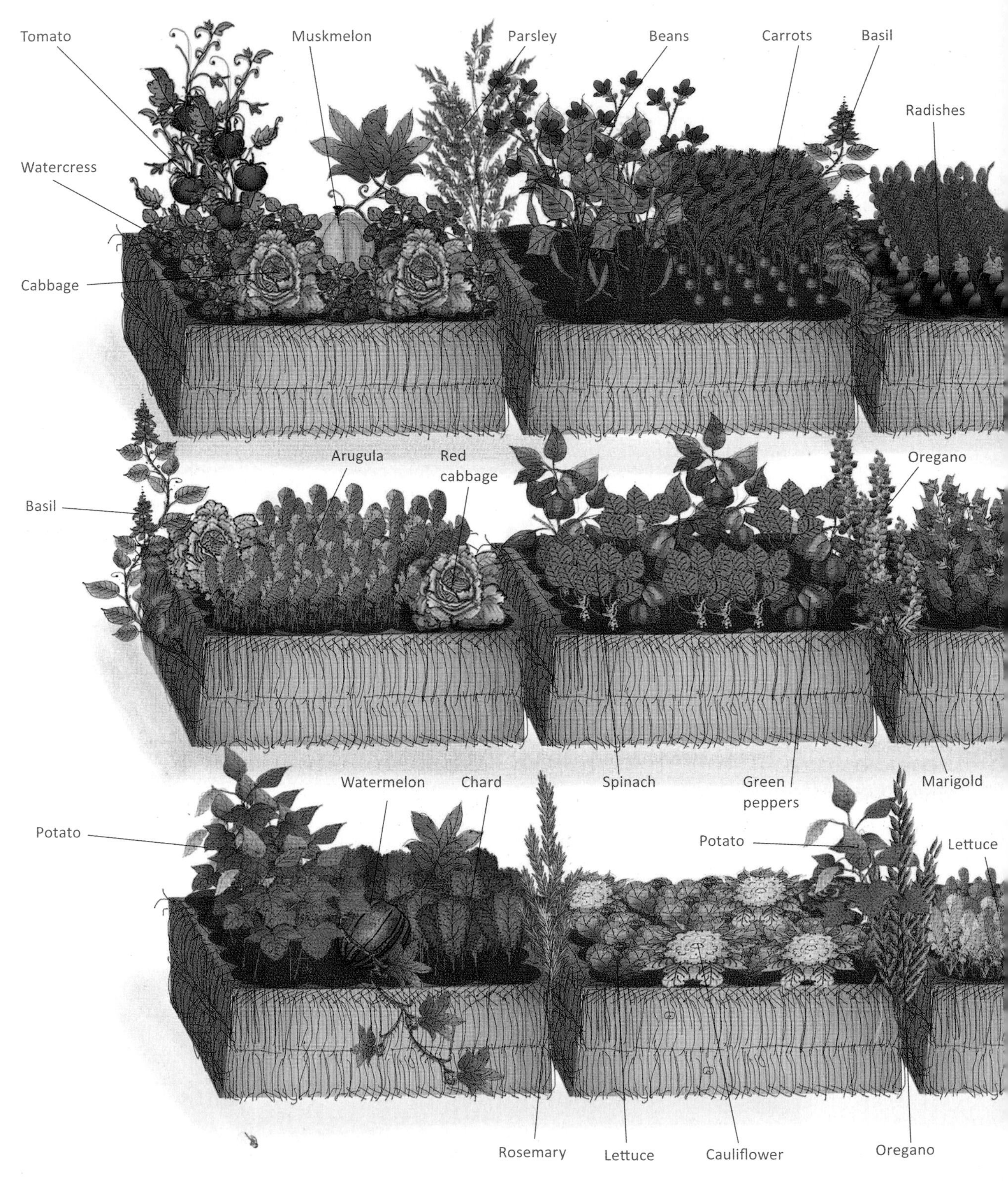

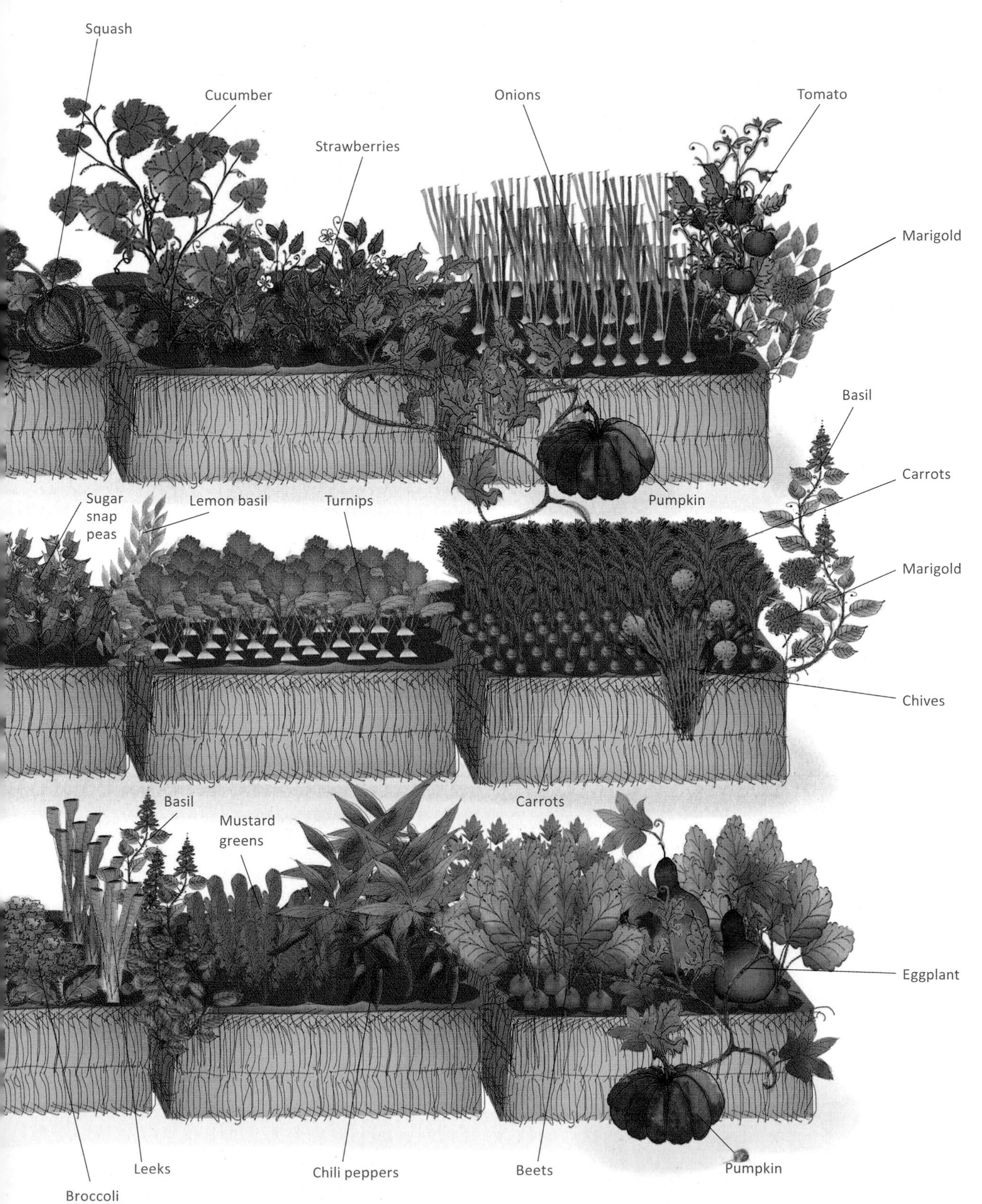
Squash
Cucumber
Strawberries
Onions
Tomato
Marigold
Basil
Pumpkin
Carrots
Sugar snap peas
Lemon basil
Turnips
Marigold
Chives
Carrots
Basil
Mustard greens
Eggplant
Broccoli
Leeks
Chili peppers
Beets
Pumpkin

TWENTY-BALE GARDEN: Layout and Suggested Plants

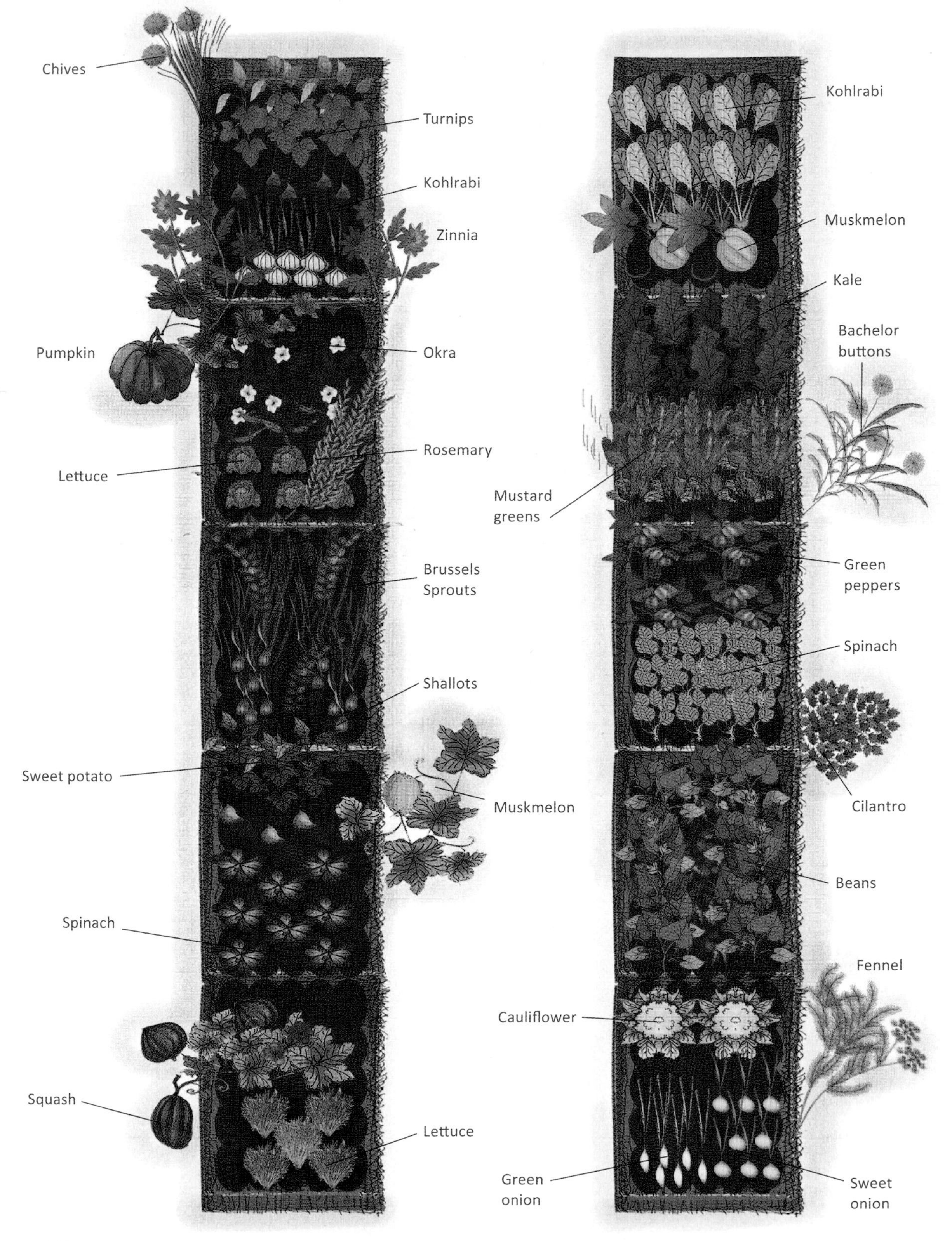

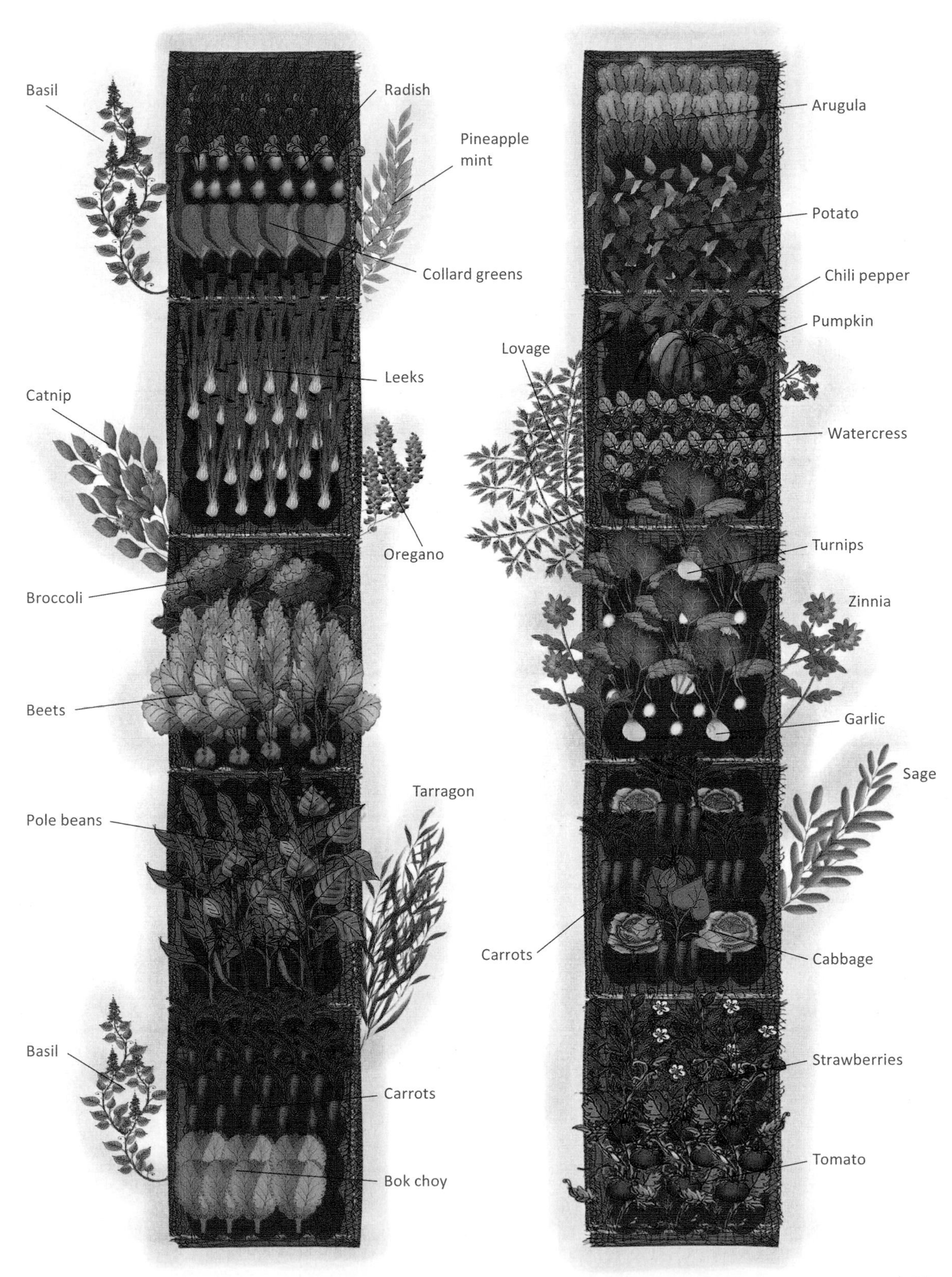
Basil
Radish
Pineapple mint
Collard greens
Leeks
Catnip
Oregano
Broccoli
Beets
Pole beans
Tarragon
Basil
Carrots
Bok choy
Arugula
Potato
Chili pepper
Pumpkin
Lovage
Watercress
Turnips
Zinnia
Garlic
Sage
Carrots
Cabbage
Strawberries
Tomato

31 gal | 117.3 L

Making YOUR OWN BALES

I RECEIVE LOTS OF FEEDBACK from Straw Bale Gardeners, and in today's world of social media it makes communicating with people all over the world as simple as a Facebook message or a tweet. Two of the most common frustrations people come to me with are: first, they can't find straw bales where they live, and second, they have so much volume of partially composted straw left over at the end of the year and they wonder what they can do with it. I'm lucky because I have easy access to straw bales and I have many other gardens where I can spread my composted straw, so neither of these issues had ever really been on my radar. A couple of years ago, I got serious about solving these two big problems for people and I am happy to announce that I have devised a simple solution.

The answer is the BaleMaker3000! This is a pet name for the very simple "machine" I've designed to easily make your own bales. To be clear, it's made from three 2 × 6 boards that are each 8 feet long, so it hardly qualifies as a real machine. New bales can then be made from leftover old bales or from other sources of compostable organic material—nearly anything that's easily accessible. These homemade bales could completely take the place of straw bales in your future gardens if you have difficulty finding traditional small straw bales. The important thing I'd like to assure you is that they really do work… extremely well, in fact. I am a bit hesitant to say it, but in many cases, I have gotten even better results from the homemade bales than from traditional straw bales. So how does this BaleMaker3000 actually work?

Opposite: Not as difficult as it looks: This little contraption I invented is easy and cheap to build, and by using it you can manufacture your own plantable bales, from last year's crumbling bales or just about any compostable organic material that's available. The secret is the compression. If the finished planting bale (above) is made from pre-composted material (such as last year's bales) it does not need conditioning and can be planted as soon as it's made.

No Tree/Post

Tree/Post

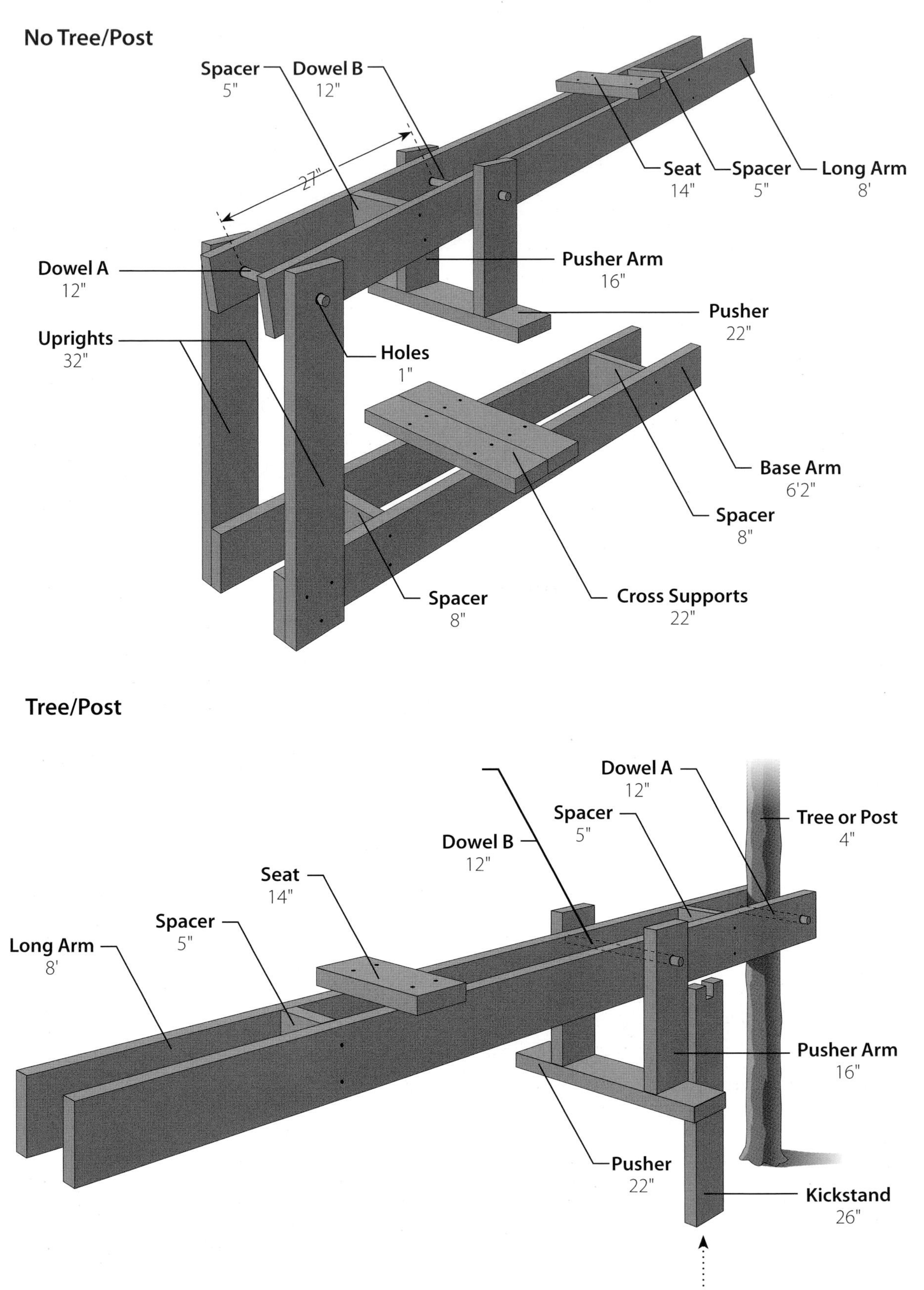

How to Build the *BaleMaker 3000*

1. Align a pair of full-length 2 x 6 boards and begin drilling the guide holes for the 1"-dia. dowels that bind the apparatus together. Locate the holes 3" from the end, centered edge to edge. Drill a second pair of holes 27" from the same end, centered.

2. Cut two pieces of 2 x 6 blocking that are equal in length to the diameter of the post or tree to which you'll be mounting the BaleMaker. If you are using a 4 x 4 post, the blocking should be 3½". Drive screws through the arms and into the blocking so they are positioned 18" and 72" from the end with the dowel holes. Drive three 3" screws at each joint.

3. Make the pushboard assembly by first cutting the pushboard support arms to 16" and the pushboard itself to 22" long. Drill 1"-dia. holes in the pushboard arms. The holes should be 2¾" from the end, centered edge to edge.

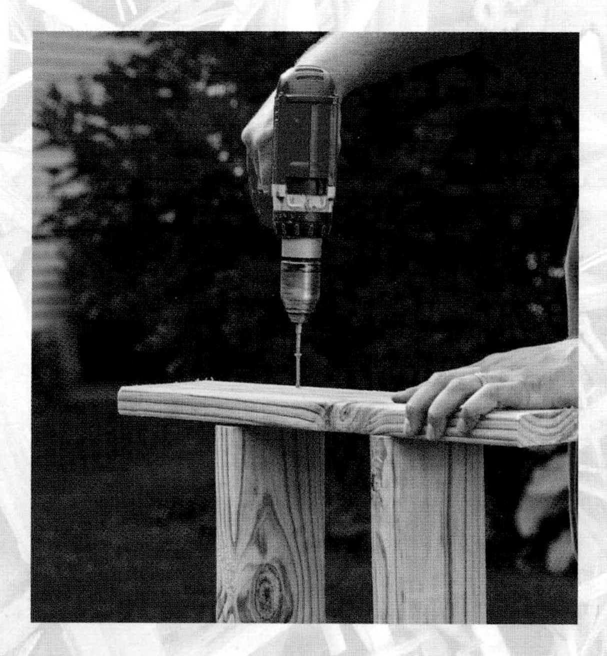

4. Attach the support arms to the pushboard so the distance between the pushboard arms equals the distance between the outside faces of the long parallel boards in the lever assembly. The holes should be on the opposite ends from the pushboard. Use three 3" screws at each joint.

(Continued)

5. Cut a 14"-long piece of 2 x 6 and attach it to the top of the lever assembly, roughly 36" in from the end opposite the pushboard. This is a seat, a little like a teeter-totter seat.

6. Cut a pair of 1"-dia. dowels so they are about 1" longer than the total width of the lever assembly.

7. Mount the pushboard to the lever assembly by aligning the 1" holes and pinning them with a dowel. Secure the joint by driving a small nail into the dowel near each end to function like a cotter pin. The pushboard assembly should be able to pivot slightly to achieve consistent compressive force when you use the BaleMaker.

8. Drill a 1"-dia. hole through the standard (a tree or post), 24" up from the ground and keep it level (inset photo). This does little harm to most trees, but I wouldn't do it to a tree that is right in the middle of my front yard. Mount the assembly to the post or tree by aligning the 1" holes and driving a 1" dowel through all parts. Pin at the end with a brad or nails as in Step 7. After you've used your new BaleMaker 3000 to create as many planting bales as you like (see pages 81 to 85), you can easily disassemble it for storage until you're ready to plant next year's bale garden.

The BaleMaker3000 is really a glorified lever, allowing you to multiply the force you create with your own weight and squish the organic mix tightly together to make a nicely compressed bale. You cannot buy a BaleMaker3000; you have to make it yourself (or get someone to make it for you), but it is really easy, so don't fret.

You're going to need about $25 to build it, unless you are a scrounger in which case you might find the materials you need in a dumpster behind a construction site. I have designed one basic model, which requires you to already have a pre-existing permanent post or tree that you can drill a hole through. A slight modification is needed if you don't have a tree or post you can use, but either way this will take no more than 20 minutes to build. For my first model, I used an 8" diameter spruce tree in my backyard, one with all the lower branches pruned away. An old basketball hoop post or clothesline pole would work fine too, as long as there is concrete holding the post down in the ground, because the force will be pulling up on the tree or post. You will need three 8-foot long 2 × 6 boards, a 3-foot length of 1" diameter wood dowel and a 25 to 40 gallon rectangular plastic storage bin (the kind you use to store your holiday decorations.)

How to Make Your Own Planting Bales

Now to use the BaleMaker, first lay two strings down inside the plastic bin. I use little strips of tape to hold the strings in place about 8" apart and let the ends hang out on each end. Fill the bin with organic matter, such as old straw, weeds pulled from your garden, kitchen scraps (compostable only, no meat, no dairy), your dead flowers from Valentine's day, small tree branches pruned over winter, grass clippings, leaves you raked and collected last fall—literally anything that you find, with few exceptions, will work well, and mixing different things together really works best. Some pine needles are okay, but only a pitchfork full per bale, as they are very acidic and the pH level of the bale will be too low if too many are used.

If you have a pile of wood mulch, you could use a pitchfork full in each bale, but again not too much because it is really slow to decompose and release nutrients. As you build layers in the bin, mix in a bit of the conditioning fertilizer every few layers. It is certainly much easier to get the fertilizer evenly distributed inside the bale now than to wait and try to wash it in from the top with your water hose later on. You can put the entire amount required for conditioning the bale into this bale. While these homemade bales will likely be slightly smaller than the straw bales you would buy, they are denser and heavier, so don't cut back on the nitrogen used. Wait to apply the Day 10 application of 10-10-10 or organic phosphorus and

Lay two lengths of twine in the bottom of your plastic bin, and use a few strips of tape to hold the string in place so it doesn't move when you load the bin.

Load the bin with whatever you've got. Mix in kitchen scraps, grass clippings, last year's leftover bales. Anything compostable, shovel it in.

potassium until the bales have been kept wet for a ten-day period.

Once you have filled the bin and used your body weight to squish it down several times, keep putting more on top, until, when squished, it is about level with the top of the bin. It may surprise you how much material will fit into the bin. The compressing action allows a large volume of material to be squeezed inside the bale.

Once compressed, sit on top of the arms on the seat, and pull up on the twine strings. It seems to work best if you make a fixed loop on one side and then pull the other end through that loop. When you get them tight, tie them off; don't worry about getting them too tight, they only need to hold for a short time. Next, you will pull this (heavy) bin filled with your new bale to the spot where you plan to grow the garden, and turn over the bin. It may take some coaxing to get it out, but once the bale is out, the strings will hold the shape nicely. This mixture of organic material will mean that much of the contents may have short stem lengths. Grass clippings, for example, would not hold together very well if you left this new bale exposed with only these two strings holding it together.

For this reason, you need to measure off a length of chicken wire and wrap the bale with it tightly. I like to buy the 24" tall chicken wire rolls and then cut the whole roll in half with a wire snips, so I have two rolls each 12" tall. (You can just buy the shorter height if you are not as frugal as I am.) I wrap the chicken wire all the way around the bale and overlap the two ends about 12". I use a 24" tall 2 × 2 post with a point cut on one end, and then staple both ends of the chicken wire to the post, starting about 6" from the pointed end.

Left: Squish down with everything you've got, then lift up and pack it full again. Repeat this until the bin is level with the top and packed tightly.

Right: Leaves, small branches, expired tulips, rotten apples—they all go in the bin. Keeping some more fibrous material on the bottom, sides, and top will help to hold the bale together.

Once the wire is firmly stapled to the post, I twist the post, hard, even using a pipe wrench or large pliers, to tighten the wire snuggly around the bale. This will squeeze the bale really tightly. Once tight, use a hammer to tap the end of the 2 × 2 into the ground and it will hold its position nicely. You could add a few more staples if you want to ensure it will not come loose. If you have questions about how to do this, you can always visit our website or our YouTube channel for Straw Bale Gardens where we have a number of videos showing the BaleMaker3000 in use. You will get the hang of it quickly and you'll be making bales like magic in no time. You will now be looking for compostable organic matter everywhere, collecting all of your own compost material, and making bales year round so they are ready for use in your next garden the upcoming spring (or fall for lucky winter gardeners in the south). It's like having little compost piles everywhere in your garden; it works so well and you will love the results.

I have even made new bales from old bales that were made in the BaleMaker3000 the year before, but after using them twice, they are really just broken down into beautiful soil. The chicken wire can be reused, just pull out the staples, and unwind the wire. I must emphasize how wonderfully these bales have worked in my experiments; some of my biggest yields over the past two years have come while testing these homemade bales, so don't be afraid to try making some yourself. Now, you are not limited to using straw, so start collecting anything that is compostable to make your next bale.

How to Make Your Own Planting Bales

1. If you're baling up undercomposed materials, mix in some fertilizer as you layer in the organic material. You won't need to try to work the fertilizer down into the bales in order to condition them later on.

2. It will astound you how much you can squeeze into that bin. Keep packing it full until it's full and you can't get it to smash down any further.

3. Tie up the strings while holding downward pressure on the arms.

4. The compacted bin will be heavy, but drag it to the location where you want to grow in that new bale next season.

5. Tip the bin over and dump it out. You may have to really shake the bin hard to get it to come out. Don't worry, the strings will temporarily hold the bale together.

6. Wrap the entire bale with chicken wire so that you have about 10" of overlap on the ends.

7. Staple the chicken wire to a short 2 x 2 about two feet long, and twist that board to wrap the chicken wire around it. A pipe wrench or large pliers will get it really snug. This twisting action will squeeze your new bale very tight, and hold it together for the entire season. Add a few more staples once the wire is tight to keep it from coming loose, and pound the end of the 2 x 2 into the ground.

Conditioning THE BALES

THE PROCESS OF GETTING YOUR STRAW BALES to compost internally to a stage at which they will support root growth is called "conditioning" and is a simple but essential part of the process in growing a Straw Bale Garden. Conditioning is directly analogous to composting. Most gardeners are familiar with the concept of composting and understand that any organic matter can be composted; however, some materials decompose more quickly than others. Wood chips from a hardwood tree, such as an oak or elm, can take several years, while composting fresh grass clippings can be completed in only a month or two. A regular compost pile is always alive with microbial activity and encouraging these microbes is as easy as turning the pile, which aerates the contents with oxygen. Wetting down the pile and incorporating nitrogen-rich fertilizer every two to three weeks will also help speed the composting process. A good balance of inputs into a compost pile can really get it cooking! In many cases a freshly turned, fed and watered compost pile will heat up, reaching temperatures of 160°F or higher. This heat normally does a thorough job of killing off harmful bacteria, such as those present in manure, and it sterilizes any weed seeds present in the compost as well. The combination of the microbial activity, heat, and worm or insect activities in a compost pile produces a rich, fertile organic media that plant roots love. Applying what many gardeners already know about composting and proper compost pile management to straw-bale gardening will help explain the methods we use in the bale conditioning process.

Opposite: Preparing the bales by "conditioning" them for about two weeks prior to planting is essential to successful Straw Bale Gardening. Part of this process involves spraying the bales to get water and fertilizer deep down inside so they can start to "cook."

A young Straw Bale Gardener helps to "condition" the bales and start the decomposition process. Get started two weeks before the target planting date. Photo courtesy Jean, Washington, IA

Get started early

The process of conditioning the bales will take approximately 10 to 12 days—the exact time required will be somewhat determined by the air temperatures. If the target planting date is May 1, then beginning the conditioning process in mid-April should allow ample time for conditioning. Refer to your calendar and count backwards two weeks from the average last frost date in your area, and this should be your target date to start the conditioning process. For those of you in warmer climates who are planning to plant a winter Straw Bale Garden, use the same two weeks of conditioning prior to your target planting date.

It is essential that you allow the bales to condition (compost) for this short time before you plant anything into them. Conditioning doesn't mean that the bales will be completely composted in twelve days; so don't expect that they will look or feel like compost inside after this 12-day process. It simply means the bales will have composted far enough that the bacteria inside is activated and has begun to digest the straw, making nitrogen and other nutrients available. Planting too early in bales that are not conditioned properly will yield very poor results, including dead transplants. The goal is to partially compost the bales, just enough to get them "cooking" before plants or seeds are introduced.

Get the bales "cooking"

Fertilizer and water are the chief ingredients used to condition the bales. Many Straw Bale Gardeners choose cheap and readily available lawn fertilizer to feed their bales. But if you prefer organic gardening techniques, you'll need to find a different food. Some organic sources of nitrogen include blood meal, feather meal or a packaged organic fertilizer such as Milorganite® (See Resources, page 172). To be clear, I use both traditional and organic methods on my straw bales and I've found that they work equally well, so I cannot offer an opinion on which is better. Lawn fertilizer is certainly less expensive and more concentrated, but it doesn't provide any other benefit over the organic nitrogen sources. By mid-season, nobody would ever be able to tell which of my bales were conditioned organically and which bales were treated with lawn fertilizer.

I only caution organic gardeners that using fresh manure of any variety is not a good idea. While the manure will have some time to decompose and compost in your garden, it may not heat-cycle enough to kill any potentially harmful bacteria. We are mainly concerned about the big E, (E-coli), which can be deadly and is often transmitted through the use of manure that is too "fresh." Chicken manure is a great source of nitrogen, but it shouldn't look or smell like manure any more if you're going to use it in your Straw Bale Garden. Well-composted manure looks and smells like rich black soil. You'll only know it is manure, because you know you started with manure. Once composted for a year you won't be able to tell by the way it looks or smells that it was manure. Supplement any manure used with organic fertilizer, as the concentration of nitrogen in the manure may not be high enough to activate the bacteria as quickly as necessary. Manure has no guaranteed analysis, so it isn't reliable as a consistent source of nitrogen. If using manure, use no more than half of the amount for each application, with the other half being the bagged organic nitrogen source.

Use a plastic container with holes punched in the lid to get a nice even distribution of fertilizer covering the entire top surface of the bale evenly.

Use a hose end sprayer to help push the fertilizer into the bales. The dry bales will absorb a lot of water the first day, when the straw is dry, but it won't take more than a couple of gallons of water during any application afterward before you'll see water running out the bottom of the bale.

Conditioning your bales

DAY ONE

Traditional Refined Lawn Fertilizer: After the bales are set in place and the rows are adjusted to their final position, the first application of nitrogen-rich lawn fertilizer should be applied. Spread ½ cup (4 ounces) of product evenly per bale. Sprinkle it all over the bale surface, side-to-side and end-to-end. Remember that virtually any high nitrogen lawn fertilizer will work well for the conditioning process, but avoid any fertilizer with herbicide (weed killer) in it.

Organic Nitrogen Sources: If you are interested in using organic gardening techniques, use three cups of your selected organic nitrogen source, blood meal, feather meal or any other organic nitrogen source you prefer. Composted chicken manure also works well mixed 50/50 with a bagged nitrogen source. The nitrogen in these fertilizers is providing a food source for the microorganisms (bacteria) that are going to do the actual work of decomposing the straw. Moisture is also a key component and is required to fuel the same microbial activity inside the bale. Water also carries the fertilizer into the bale. Use a hose end sprayer to really push the fertilizer down into the bale until the fertilizer seems to have soaked in and until the bale is thoroughly waterlogged and water is running out the bottom. It can take awhile to wash the organic fertilizer into the bale, so be patient and let the water do its magic as it dissolves the chunks and carries it inside the bale to the waiting bacteria. They will use the nitrogen introduced as a food source to grow their population quickly until they have reached a high level inside the bales. It is only then that they will begin to digest the straw and give off nitrogen and other nutrients as byproducts.

THE MANURE PERPLEX

A very common question I get is whether it is advisable to use manure in a Straw Bale Garden. My advice is yes; as long as it is well-composted manure (especially poultry manure), it can be used successfully. Well-composted means that it has completely broken down. The manure must have been heated up during the composting process so any weed seeds are sterilized and any E-Coli bacteria are killed by the heat. If the manure pile is sprouting weeds, you can guess what will happen if you spread this manure on top of your bales. It is very difficult to estimate how much nitrogen is actually contained in composted manure, so I encourage the use of composted manure as a supplement to one of the other organic sources with a measured guaranteed analysis on the bag. It is only when manure has completely composted (finished) that it is safe to use on vegetable crops.

DAY TWO

All that is needed is to water the bales again and ensure they are completely saturated. Using "warm" rainwater or water collected the previous day in buckets is a good habit to get into. Water from a faucet tends to be rather cold, and cold water tends to slow down the microbial activity inside the bale. A cold shower tends to slow down reproduction in many species.

Tip

Watering your bales can involve some creativity. Here, the gardener has not installed a soaker hose yet, so he rigged up a straight-line sprinkler over the bales.

DAY THREE

Sprinkle another ½ cup of the same fertilizer as on day one (or three cups of the organic) and wash the fertilizer into the bale with "warm" water.

DAY FOUR

Another water-only day, again to full saturation. It will not take much "warm" water, about 1 to 2 gallons per bale and you will have water running out the bottom of each bale almost immediately.

DAY FIVE

Sprinkle another ½ cup of fertilizer (or 3 cups of the organic) on each bale and wash it in with more "warm" water.

DAY SIX

"Warm" water only! By now it is likely that a sweet aroma will begin to emit from the bales. Reassure any concerned neighbors that this smell dissipates quickly. Slip your hand or an old meat thermometer inside one or more of the bales and you will experience a slightly elevated temperature. You can also tip a bale over and feel underneath. This is the beginning of the bacteria "cooking" inside the bale. This decomposition process will generate a significant amount of heat, but for now a slight increase should be felt and smelled. If not, don't worry. It just means your temperatures may have been a bit too low to get much bacteria growth going just yet. Stay on track, finish the conditioning as directed, and everything will work out just fine. It always does.

DAYS SEVEN, EIGHT, AND NINE

Apply ¼ cup of fertilizer (or 1½ cups of the organic) to each bale each day followed by "warm" watering to wet the bales every day. These three days are typically the most active days for the bacteria development in the bales. Much depends on air temperatures

THE SMELL TEST

Grandma Josephine always said, "If manure still smells or looks like manure, then it isn't ready to use just yet." The pile should look and smell like good black soil—this will indicate that it has broken down and has "finished." It is only when manure has completely composted that it is safe to use on vegetable crops.

Applying so much water to a bale of straw often causes them to expand and shrink, creating "cracks" in the bale. You should fill in any of these cracks with clean compost, straw or sterile planting mix. Try to keep the fertilizer you apply from washing right down through any cracks, because it won't be very effective if it is applied to the soil below the bale.

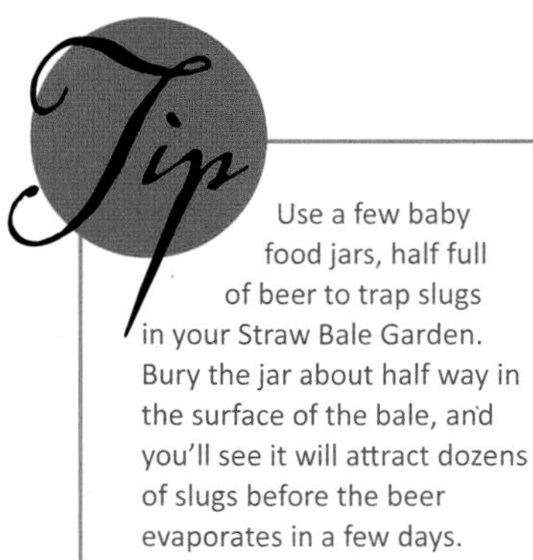

Tip

Use a few baby food jars, half full of beer to trap slugs in your Straw Bale Garden. Bury the jar about half way in the surface of the bale, and you'll see it will attract dozens of slugs before the beer evaporates in a few days.

during this time, but don't fret—even if the bales are not "warm" to the touch, there is plenty of bacteria growth happening inside. It is common for the bales to get 10 to 40 degrees hotter inside the bales than air temperature readings outside on the same day. This means the bales are really "cooking," and the bacteria party is in full swing inside the bales. If you are using blood meal or feather meal for conditioning, you may notice flies and other insects buzzing around the bales. They are after the fertilizer, because remember it is simply organic matter that is high in nitrogen, so the flies love to eat it as well. The flies will go away once the fertilizer has decomposed a bit and washed down inside the bales.

DAY TEN

Apply one cup per bale of a balanced 10-10-10 type general garden fertilizer. **TIP:** If you have an old bag of garden fertilizer left over in your garage or garden shed, but it's gotten hard or chunky, bust up the chunks and use up what you have. Do not worry if it is not exactly 10-10-10. Our main focus here is to get some P and K (Phosphorus and Potassium) worked into the bales interior so it penetrates into the root zone. Double-check to make sure the fertilizer doesn't have any herbicide or weed killer in it. Organic gardeners will use 3 cups of an equivalent organic source of phosphorus and potassium. Consider using bone meal or fish meal for the phosphorus mixed with 50% wood ashes, a great source for potassium (aka potash).

A few "water slides" or cracks will have developed in the bales, as the water tends to create these paths of least resistance through the bales. They simply look like little channels down through the bales. Fill in any large cracks in the bales with straw or sterile planting mix. Don't fill these cracks with soil from your garden—you will introduce weed seeds and soil-borne problems we are trying to avoid by using the bales. Try to spray water into the areas around these cracks to get the fertilizer down into the interior of the bales without allowing it to wash into these channels and quickly out the bottom of the bale.

Mushrooms may sprout on the outside of the bales, and this is a good sign. Mushroom are a sign that the inside of the bales have begun to decompose. The mushrooms that bloom will not hurt anything, so there is no need to do anything to them. Knock them over if you'd like, but they will probably grow right back. If you ignore them, they will disappear completely within a few weeks.

Mushrooms blooming on the outside of the bales are a great sign that the inside of the bale is decomposing nicely. Mushrooms in this case are NOT good to eat, but they are not harmful in any way to you or the garden. There is no need to do anything to them; just plant around them and you'll see they will disappear within a few weeks just as quickly as they popped up.

DAY ELEVEN

Get your bedding plants from the nursery, or purchase your planting mix and seeds, or just take a day off and relax.

WORMS

Worms are wonderful in a garden because they help break down the complex organic material back into essential elements that are soluble and can be easily taken up by plant roots. Do not be surprised to see an accumulation of earthworms in the straw bales, as they enjoy this nutrient-rich decomposing organic matter. This decomposing straw bale is like a five-star hotel for worms, and worms mean one thing—worm castings. Believe it or not, worm castings are a good thing! They are extremely rich in soluble and available micronutrients that have been transformed through the worms' digestive process into a form that can be easily absorbed by plant roots. We rely on insects, worms and bacteria to do the vast majority of decomposition work on the planet. If it weren't for bacteria, insects and worms that keep eating, digesting and decomposing dead organic matter, the entire surface of the earth would be covered with a thick layer of dead organic material such as bones, trees and animal carcasses. Thank an ant, a worm or a bacteria for the fine job they do every day.

Don't expect after the 12 day conditioning period that the inside of the bale will look like compost or planting mix: it will not. Inside the bales you may see little black specks that resemble pepper, and these specks are the beginnings of the creation of what we might later recognize as soil.

DAY TWELVE TO EIGHTEEN

What now exists inside the straw bales is a nutrient-rich, slightly composted organic media that is much warmer than surrounding air and soil temperatures as it is still "cooking." It is weed- and disease-free; it is full of worms and bacteria; and it has good particle structure that holds plenty of moisture but drains excess water easily. In simpler terms, it is a plant seedlings' paradise, so start planting! The inside of the bales will not yet have changed in appearance, but be assured it is ready to plant. If one looks carefully inside the straw bale, it appears as if someone has sprinkled pepper inside, with tiny black specks everywhere. This is the early stage development of compost or "soil." It is important that the bacteria population has progressed enough to begin digesting the straw and giving back nitrogen. Do not expect the inside of the bales to look like finished compost or planting mix; most assuredly it will still look like straw. It will continue to produce heat as it continues to "cook," and this heat will be utilized in our Straw Bale "Greenhouse" to help seeds germinate quickly. Seedlings will flourish in the warm bales during this early season when night time temps can be very cool.

Will these decomposing bales hurt me or make me sick?

Now that the straw has started to sprout mushrooms and decompose, it may show some signs on the outside of mold development. It is common for people to wonder if the bales can somehow be harmful to them or their children since they may get some white mold on the outside. In short, the answer is no, but with that said, anyone who is highly allergic to mold may want to consult their doctor before getting too close. Doctors have suggested to me that since the bales are not in an enclosed area, and the wind carries most spores away immediately when they bloom, it shouldn't be much of a concern. The mushrooms also reproduce from airborne spores, but they are much less problematic than mold spores. We should all be concerned about any prolonged exposure to certain molds, like black mold, in an enclosed environment like our home or our schools, but outside it is less of an issue. The plants will not absorb the mold and cannot pass it along in the fruits. Normally the mold doesn't last very long, because the straw decomposes so quickly it usually doesn't allow much time for mold growth. Go ahead and plant right over the top of any mold and don't worry. Make sure you wash any fruits or leaves that may have come in contact with any mold in the garden when you harvest, though. I know some people are sensitive to mold, so I am not intending to make light of the concerns, but every great brick of aged cheese I love to eat is always covered in mold, and it tastes so good!

At-a-glance Conditioning summary chart

*All volumes and quantities are per bale

DAY IN PROCESS	TRADITIONAL FERTILIZER	ORGANIC FERTILIZER	WATER
Day 1	½ cup	3 cups	Water to saturation
Day 2	Skip	Skip	Water to saturation
Day 3	½ cup	3 cups	Water to wash in fertilizer
Day 4	Skip	Skip	Water to saturation
Day 5	½ cup	3 cups	Water, warm is best
Day 6	Skip	Skip	Water, warm is best
Day 7	¼ cup	1 ½ cups	Water, warm is best
Day 8	¼ cup	1 ½ cups	Water, warm is best
Day 9	¼ cup	1 ½ cups	Water, warm is best
Day 10	1 cup 10-10-10	3 cups with P and K	Water to wash in fertilizer
Day 12	PLANT TODAY	Wait 5 more days	Water any new plantings

Soaker hoses should go in before planting

Lay the soaker hoses down so they run down the center on top of each bale in your garden. Use some 20-inch lengths of your 14-gauge wire to make big staples to hold the hose in position in the middle of each row of bales. If you have more than 40 bales in your garden you may need two separate soaker hose zones from your main hose. You would then also need separate hose end timers for each zone. It is much easier to get this soaker hose in place ahead of time, than it is to try to lay it down when everything is planted. If you can program an alarm clock the hose end timer will be simple, and now you can jump on the plane without gardening worries. No traditional soil gardener could ever leave town like this during the heat of summer. If heavy rain fell while they were away, and in addition their automatic soaker hose came on, there would surely be a flood in the garden and dire consequences. This isn't a concern when you are a Straw Bale Gardener, because any excess water simply runs out through the bale and onto the ground. It is impossible to flood out a Straw Bale Garden.

Use some lengths of wire to hold the soaker hose in place in the center on top of each row of bales. The hose should be in place before you start planting, as it is much easier to plant around the hose, than to put the hose in around the plants.

Organic STRAW BALE GARDENS

GARDENING IN A COMPLETELY ORGANIC ENVIRONMENT is essential to some people. This is not a book that is meant to convince you whether or not maintaining an organic garden should be your priority. But the fact is that for many people it is a priority, so offering some additional information regarding Straw Bale Gardening organically is important.

If your intention is to grow completely organic vegetables, you must start by using only organically grown straw bales, or by making your own bales (see previous chapter: Make Your Own Bales). Finding organic straw bales can be more difficult, but it's certainly not impossible. A bit of investigation can quickly lead you to a source. Many state agriculture departments maintain a list of organic farmers and what crops they each grow in an effort to help these farmers market their crops as certified organically grown, and some of these crops are small grains. The lists are usually made public and promoted on the state's website. Oats, wheat, and barley are frequently grown organically for the production of organic flour, for which there is a very large market. These growers are thus producing the byproduct of organic straw. However, most will simply sell their straw crop as a traditional straw, since it is primarily used for animal bedding material and the organic quality normally does not add any value since the animals don't consume the straw. I have found many instances where

Opposite: Organic straw looks exactly like conventional straw of course, but if you want your SBG to be 100 percent organic you'll want to start with straw that has not been treated with herbicides or pesticides. A small grain farmer whose crop is used in the production of organic flour can also sell the straw from that harvest as organic, and usually they sell the bales at about the same price as conventional.

A few of the more common organic fertilizers include bloodmeal, bonemeal, and fishmeal. Many organic fertilizer packagers sell blended products. All of these have sufficient nitrogen content to condition bales. Most are in the 3 to 5 percent nitrogen range. Bloodmeal, however, has 12 to 15 percent nitrogen so it does a great job of getting your bales conditioned and ready to plant.

farmers sell organic straw bales for the same price as regular bales, so it will benefit you to ask around if you want to start with organic straw. It is interesting to note that most small grain crops these days are grown with very little use of herbicides or insecticides. This is mainly due to the fact that the modern hybrids of small grains are resistant to pests, and other rotation crops allow much better weed control these days. With fewer weeds already present, a field rotated to small grains typically doesn't require much, if any, herbicide.

If a straw bale does come from a source that you are concerned may have been treated with herbicide and you are afraid that herbicide may be lingering in the straw, you can send it off to be tested by a laboratory. However, it is fairly easy to test the straw yourself at home to determine if any herbicide is present. Take about one-half gallon of the intended use straw and chop it up so the individual straws are no more than ½" long. Use ten 3 to 4" clean planting containers with saucers, and fill five of these pots two-thirds full of standard clean potting mix purchased from the store. Then, add a 50/50 mix of potting mix and chopped straw to the other five pots. Now plant two small tomato seedlings in each of the different mixes. Plant three pea, three bean, and ten carrot seeds separately in one pot of each mix and water the pots well. Put the entire pot and saucer inside a plastic bag or cover with clear plastic wrap. Keep them all around 70 to 72 degrees Fahrenheit and maintain the moisture level. Wait 14 to 21 days and evaluate. If the seeds germinate well and the leaves do not curl, deform, or look discolored or pale, then your straw is clean. If you can see differences in the leaves and germination rates vary between the two mixes, avoid using those straw bales. This is a simple bioassay test, and the basic technique has been used for many years to do quick testing, as beans, peas, carrots and tomatoes are all very sensitive to the presence of different types of commonly used herbicides. This test is handy for compost, manure, foreign soils, or any growing media that you plan to bring into your garden, and if you have any reason to believe it may contain "bad stuff," test it first.

Condition of Organic Bales

Once you've established that you are working with 100 percent organic bales, the next step is to condition the bales using an organic source of nitrogen (as opposed to the lawn fertilizer I use to condition my conventional SBGs). My organic fertilizer of choice for conditioning straw bales is blood meal, which has 12 to 15 percent total nitrogen. It's great stuff, but it can be a little stinky and it's relatively expensive. It can also be difficult to get this organic fertilizer (which requires more volume than the lawn fertilizer) worked into the straw bales. But make sure you do not skimp on whichever conditioning agent you use or the bacteria in the bales will not develop enough to properly condition the straw into "soil." One trick for introducing the conditioning agent into your bales is to use a length of 2 × 2 board and a hammer to make some 3- to 8"-deep holes in the bales, and then dump the fertilizer evenly into the holes. Make a new set of six or eight holes every time you need to apply the fertilizer on days 1-3-5 and 7-8-9 during the conditioning process; this prevents a layer of dry fertilizer from building up on top of the bales. This also will keep the flies down, diminish objectionable odors, and allow the bacteria easier access to the nitrogen so it can do its job more efficiently.

If you are accustomed to getting your fertilizer the old fashioned way—with a pitch fork—I would caution you that the nitrogen content in most manure is just too low to do an effective job of activating the bacteria in your straw bales quickly. It is difficult to get the volume of manure worked into a bale so that enough nitrogen would be available for the bacteria to properly colonize the bale in time for spring planting. If manure or other weaker sources of nitrogen are used, it may be July before the bales are really ready to plant. I love manure as much as the next gardener, but sometimes it isn't practical, and conditioning bales is one of those times. The only exception is with poultry manure, which can contain 5 percent or more active nitrogen if you get the manure when it is seasoned, but not leached out. Nitrogen is soluble, so when a manure pile gets rained on over and over it will quickly lose much of its nitrogen content. Find poultry manure, not mixed with wood shavings or straw, which has been composted for six to twelve weeks and covered with plastic if outdoors during that composting period, to avoid leaching. This is "prime-time poop," and it will work well to condition your bales. If the manure is too young, it will still be really smelly and it may still contain bad bacteria like E-coli or Salmonella which we DO NOT want to introduce into our vegetable garden. The only way to be certain the manure has at least 5 percent active nitrogen is to have it tested. A simple manure nutrient content analysis from your nearest agriculture extension service soil testing lab will do the job just fine. Go to their website and follow the instructions they give for sending in a manure sample; the cost is usually under $20, with results in two or three days.

Now that we have organically conditioned organic straw bales, we need to find organically grown bedding plants, or start our own

To help granular fertilizers penetrate deep into the bales, drive a wood stake into the bales with a mallet, creating holes that are 3 to 8" deep (top). Pour the granular organic fertilizer into the holes (bottom), using a tube as a funnel if you wish.

Give your bales an organic boost

In-season fertilization will give your bales an all-organic energy boost. If you see any sign of leaves yellowing, especially during the rapid leaf production and flowering period, don't wait long to apply a liquid fertilizer. Many organic formulations are available that are soluble and can be easily applied and quickly absorbed by nutrient-deficient plants. Kelp-based liquid fertilizers are effective, and they contain many micronutrients as well. Fish emulsion is another option I like, but it stinks (literally), so plan on tossing your clothes after you apply it. If you use dry, granular fertilizer, plan on the fact that it can take weeks for the nitrogen content to be mineralized by the bacteria in the bales so it becomes available for root absorption, and by then your plants could look pretty dismal. Most of the nutrients your plants need are provided directly by the composting straw, so it is rare that lots of supplemental fertilization is needed. But if you see signs, act quickly.

seeds at home. This is pretty simple; just be aware when shopping for plants that while many bedding plant seedlings will be labeled as organically grown, many others will not be. You also want to avoid shopping at a greenhouse that is watering everything with their "magic blue water," if your objective is organic. Many organic potting mixes are available these days, so if you plan to start seeds at home or plant directly on top of your straw bales, get a bag of organic potting mix. Using your own compost is an option but buying a sterile mix will prevent contamination of the seedbed with weed seeds or disease spores, and other problems that may come with your compost.

Organic Pest Control

Pest control when gardening organically can be challenging and frustrating, but the key is persistence and quick response. Straw Bale Gardens tend to have fewer insect issues than in-ground gardens. Keep in mind that any insect or disease problems that plagued last year's soil garden can harbor over winter in the soil and reappear the following year. Because your straw bales are a brand new source of "soil," no carry-over of problems will occur. If you do experience pest problems, start treatment immediately upon detection. For example, look for eggs left in neat little rows by squash bugs on the back side of developed leaves early in the summer, and if you see them, simply remove them and you'll squash any future problems. If you see a few aphids, attack them early with a sprayer nozzle from your hose; encourage or release native parasites or predators such as aphid midges, lady beetles, or lacewings; try covering young plants with a floating row cover (see the Straw Bale Greenhouse chapter); spray hot-pepper or garlic repellents; and for the more severe infestations, apply insecticidal soap, Neem or horticultural oil. Be persistent and continue daily applications until you see little or no sign of the pests. Aphids really suck, literally, and they multiply like flies…because they are flies. If you spot leaf eaters like caterpillars or cutworms, treat by spraying with *B.t. (Bacillus thuringiensis)* or hand pick them. The floating row covers may also help with these as well.

Use insecticidal soaps if you spot Japanese beetles; I'm now convinced the pheromone traps simply attract more beetles than they trap, and I've found that shaking the beetles off or blasting them with insecticidal soap every morning does the trick pretty well. It really is only about three weeks per season when they are bad, so being persistent pays off. Most organic pest control methods recommended for traditional soil gardens will also work just fine in your Straw Bale Garden. Don't give up the battle, it isn't easy, but nothing worth doing ever is.

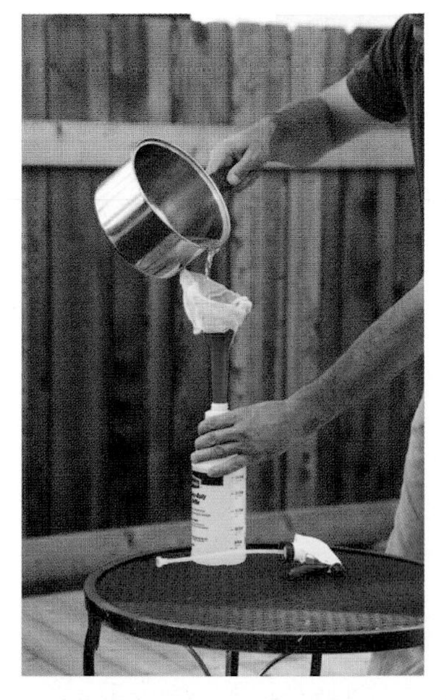

You can make your own organic pesticides for treating insect problems. One effective approach is to boil garlic and cayenne pepper in water then strain it through cheesecloth and into a spray bottle once it cools.

When spraying plants, be sure to spray the undersides of the leaves, where many pests like to hide. Spray every day or so, and as soon as possible right after rainfall.

Planting SEEDS AND SEEDLINGS

IF YOU ARE PLANNING to use prestarted transplants from the garden center, or your own seedlings started earlier under indoor grow lights, it is time to begin transplanting them into the bales. Vegetables that are considered warm-season crops, such as tomatoes, peppers, melons, eggplant, cucumber or squash, are all examples of plants with a good track record as transplants. The climate where you live (and thus the length of the growing season) will determine whether or not you must start with transplants or if you can start with seeds. If you would normally use transplants, then purchase the smaller-sized transplants; they are less costly and the extra warmth generated in the root zone by the "cooking" straw bale will encourage very rapid early season growth. Your tiny transplants will quickly surpass the much bigger transplants that your neighbor uses in the traditional soil garden on the other side of your fence. Keep in mind that your transplants are going into a root zone that will be approximately 85° on average, whereas the soil may be only 50° or 55° on the same date.

Use your hand trowel to stab into the bale and make a hole by working the straw back and forth. Sometimes it is necessary to remove a little straw to make the hole for the transplants.

Opposite: Seedlings may be planted directly into a hole in the straw bale. Seeds require a layer of sterile planting mix for germination.

Dig right in

Move the soaker hose slightly to the side and use a hand trowel to stab into the bale. Working back and forth, open up an area large enough to insert the entire root mass easily without breaking up the roots. If necessary, remove a small amount of straw to accommodate the root ball. If the bale is really tight, use a pair of pliers to pull a little straw out to make room.

Internal bale heat

Make sure the bales are not too hot for planting seedlings. If a meat thermometer stuck 6 inches into the top of a bale reads over 105°, then wait another day or two until it cools down before planting. If you don't have a thermometer, push your hand inside the bale before planting into it and if the bale feels hot on your skin, it is probably over 105°. If it feels like warm bath water or cooler, then it is safe to go ahead and plant your transplants that day. Temperatures don't matter at all when you are seeding the bale, so go ahead and plant seeds any time after Day 12, regardless of how hot the bale is.

I like to always remove the pot, even the peat pots that are supposed to magically disappear after planting but don't. Any resistance to root development on a young transplant can only be detrimental, so carefully remove even the peat pots.

Remove all pots

Make certain to remove the pot, and even if it is a "peat-pot" it should still be removed. I find that the peat-pot can inhibit root growth for young transplants. Always cut the pot away; do not try to shake a plant from the pot because this can loosen or damage the tender roots. Young vegetable transplants are particularly vulnerable to rough treatment, tearing up the roots can slow the development of the young plant significantly. Be gentle with them, and don't ever allow any exposed roots to dry out. Move them quickly into the bale, and then add a dose of water.

Healing in transplants

Use a handful of sterile planting mix to cover any exposed roots and to fill in the planting hole you made in the bale. DO NOT USE SOIL from your nearby garden for this purpose of healing in transplants. Introducing soil to the surface of our straw bales will introduce weed seeds, possible soil borne disease or other pathogens to this previously "sterile" straw bale.

Sterile planting mix should be used to "heal in" around transplants, assuring that the roots are well covered and not exposed to the air.

Planting mix on top for a seedbed

When planting cool-season crops (such as peas, beans, carrots, lettuce), the seeds must be planted in a layer of planting mix on the surface of the bales. This planting mix will hold moisture, and keep the seeds in position as they germinate and eventually grow roots down into the bale itself. Create this seedbed with sterile planting mix (do not use soil) on top of the bales. Planting mix often has some slow-release fertilizer mixed into it already, which will provide nutrients to young seedlings after they germinate. Mound up the planting mix on top of the bales, and tamp down the mix to create a 1- to 2-inch flat layer from edge to edge and from end to end of the bale.

Below: Mound up the planting mix on top of the bales, right over the top of the soaker hose, and use a piece of board to pat down the planting mix, so it creates a 1- to 2-inch-thick layer on top of each bale. Keep the planting layer all the way to the edges and to the end of each bale.

Water newly planted seedlings to assure the roots are sealed in and will not be exposed to air. Exposed roots can dry out quickly and cause severe transplant shock.

Seed packet wisdom

Read the back of the seed packet to determine the proper depth for planting and the recommended seed spacing. Recommendations are likely to vary greatly between vegetables (and even seed companies) and can also vary between different varieties of the same vegetable. A planting guide is also provided for many of the most common vegetables in a plant spacing chart at the end of this chapter. Always seed in a checkerboard pattern using the "in the row" spacing recommended on the seed packet as a guide. It is necessary to thin any sprouted seeds to the desired density by snipping off all but one of the seedlings in a single spot with a sharp scissors. This works particularly well with carrots and other tiny seeds like lettuce and spinach where getting just one seed in each planting hole is nearly impossible. The seedbed on top of the Straw Bale Garden where these seeds will be planted will be toasty warm, so once germinated, the seedlings will grow very rapidly. Many crops can be successively seeded throughout the summer, so once the leaf lettuce, for example, has been harvested a couple of times you can pull out the roots and replant seeds immediately. Same goes for most other greens like collards, mustard, Swiss chard, spinach and kale. Replanting is also an option for peas, broccoli, cauliflower, beets, green onions, cabbage and many others. Replant seeds the same day you are harvesting or even a week before you'll harvest, and a second crop will be ready before the season is over.

Storing seeds for the next planting

It is not necessary to use every seed you purchase right away. If you have leftover seeds, they will keep best in an airtight container in the refrigerator. It is wise to add a silica gel pack (desiccant) or a couple teaspoons of powdered milk wrapped in a paper towel with tape to keep it from going everywhere. This will keep the seeds dry and cool, which will extend their viable life dramatically. After about three or four years you might want to toss the seeds and buy new ones because the germination rate will have gone down significantly. Date each seed pack when you put it into the plastic storage container, so you'll know how old they are and when you need to trash them.

Mother Nature can be frosty

It has become tradition for me to plant my garden up to two weeks prior to the "normal" planting date where I am located in Minnesota. I will not venture to give you a planting date because it varies, of course, depending on your latitude and your local climate. I can tell you that with a Straw Bale Garden you can plan to plant up to

Making "seed tape" from paper towels will save lots of time in the spring. Spacing will be perfect, and this means no thinning once the seeds germinate. It is much easier to see those tiny seeds with a white paper towel behind them than it is with potting mix under them. This works great for people with big clumsy fingers like mine.

MAKING PAPER TOWEL "SEED TAPE" FOR YOUR STRAW BALE GARDEN

When the long winter has given you the blues, this is a fun and useful project that will save you time in the spring. Use a roll of single-ply (pull apart double-ply) paper towels to make "seed tape" that can be unrolled in the garden on planting day in the spring, for perfect seed spacing. Mix equal parts of flour and water, and with a tiny craft brush paint splotches of the "paste" on the paper towel in a grid pattern. Each paste splotch will hold a single seed so this is when you can determine the exact spacing the plants will have in the spring. It is much easier to use a tweezers here to get exactly one seed on each spot. It may help to slide some graph paper under your paper towel to keep the seeds evenly spaced. Make sure to put seeds all the way to the edges of the paper towel as the surface of your bale will be slightly wider than the paper towel. Remember to measure the length of your straw bales, so you know how long to make your paper towel seed tapes. Once the seeds are in place cover the whole thing with another layer of paper towel, and press them together. When they dry the seeds will be fixed in place between the two layers. Label the paper towel with the type of seed used and roll it up to store somewhere cool and dry until planting day.

two weeks or more prior to the date you would normally venture to get out into the garden to plant. The reason we are able to plant into a Straw Bale Garden so much earlier is entirely due to the "greenhouse" we will erect immediately after planting. More on the "greenhouse" in the chapter called "Straw Bale Greenhouse."

Simply unroll the paper towel seed tape on top of an inch of planting mix, and then cover with enough mix to bury the seeds tape at the proper depth, as recommended on the seed packet. Water everything well after seeding, and you will see the paper towel disappear in a short time as it dissolves away.

Planting seeds on top of a warm straw bale that has now been "cooking" for two weeks is a quick and easy task. Use sterile planting mix to create a seedbed 1 to 2 inches thick, and plant into that seedbed. DO NOT USE REGULAR GARDEN SOIL, or you'll end up introducing lots of weed seeds and other soil-borne diseases and problems that our Straw Bale Garden is designed to avoid.

Tip

A HANDY PLANTING AIDE

I have found that by using a variety of free plant trays from the garden center, I can make an imprint in the planting surface creating a pattern that makes spacing seeds very precise. Seed spacing is one key to getting a healthy stand of most crops.

Earliest plantings

Because they are less susceptible to being damaged by light frost, plant these vegetables first and as early as possible once the bales are conditioned: Broccoli, Brussels sprouts, Cabbage, Collard, Garlic, Horseradish, Kale, Kohlrabi, Leek, Onion, Pea, Radish, Shallot, Spinach and Turnips. Make sure you provide frost protection if temperatures dip too low. These plants are tough, but 20° temperatures will do almost any of us in pretty quickly.

Later crops

Wait to plant these vegetables, as they are more susceptible to even a light frost: Beets, Carrots,Cauliflower, Celery, Chard, Chinese Cabbage, Endive, Lettuce, Mustard, Parsnip, Potato, and Swiss Chard. The sheet plastic covers for your SBG will normally allow these to begin at least two weeks earlier than normal. Since many of these greens will be ready to harvest three to four weeks after seeding, you may have the earliest fresh lettuce around.

After any risk of frost, plant these

The following vegetables are normally planted when it gets warm, but the temperature in the bales and under the straw bale greenhouse will be plenty warm by the local last frost date: Cantaloupe, Cucumber, Eggplant, Lima Bean, New Zealand Spinach, Pepper, Pumpkin, Snap Bean, Squash, Sweet Potato, Tomato and Watermelon. Keep them protected if the temperatures are even in the 30° range, just in case, because these are most sensitive to cold.

Bottom left: Strawberries can be treated as annuals and planted early into the bale. They establish quickly and will be prolific even the same season they were planted.

Bottom right: A row of annual flowers planted into the side of some of the bales in your Straw Bale Garden will make the garden a stand-out hit with neighbors. Pretty as well as productive, a skirt always dresses things up.

Tip

PREDICTABILITY IS KEY TO PLANNING

If you ever move to a different part of the world, learning how to work with the local soils can take some adjustment. Luckily, if you are a Straw Bale Gardener, all you need to do is locate a few bales of straw and you're back in business. Each year, no matter where you are, if you follow the same conditioning process using a bale of straw, the resulting planting media inside the bale is essentially the same, and your results will be very predictable. If you usually dedicate one bale to 60 carrots and one tomato plant, then the same size bale should produce a similar amount of production. Add or subtract bales to produce more or less of any particular crop.

It just might grow, so give it a go

There are certainly other crops not mentioned here that are worth trying—go ahead! The Straw Bale Garden growing environment is very favorable to virtually every crop. The conditioned bale has adequate fertility, a balanced Ph, plenty of moisture, and a well-drained root zone creating plenty of air spaces allowing for quick root development—truly an environment where virtually any young plant will thrive.

It's not that these won't grow but . . .

Stay away from those crops that physically do not make much sense to grown in bales, like sweet corn. You would be doing well to get two stalks of corn in a bale with the huge roots they produce. That would result in perhaps four ears of corn from a whole bale, and that is not a wise investment of money or time. Avoid those crops that come back from the same mother-root stock every year, like asparagus, artichokes and rhubarb. Keep in mind the bale will decompose completely within a couple of years, so those perennial-type vegetable roots would need to be transplanted to another bale, and they do not like to be transplanted so often. They need time to develop in the place where they have been planted for several years before they will really begin to thrive. Strawberries are a perennial rooted crop, but they are a bit different.

Strawberries . . . that's "straw" berries

Strawberries grow like mad in straw, and while it isn't exactly how they got their name, it sure could be, because they do love growing in straw bales.They establish roots fast and are prolific immediately, so buying new plants each spring is an inexpensive yet productive option. Strawberries are much easier to tend and harvest when planted up on the bales, making it worth the small investment in new plants each spring. Many gardeners think of strawberries as perennial growers, which they are for most of the country. Thus they can be overwintered and transplanted into new bales in the spring if you want to go through the work of transplanting them twice. Strawberries will even send runners to other bales trying to set roots for new plants. Guide the runners back to the mother bale or chop them off because they will "run" up to two or three bales away if left alone.

A skirt always dresses up the garden

Credit for the idea to plant annual flowers into the sides of the bales actually goes to my mother. While she always liked the Straw Bale

Garden, she was never a big fan of decomposing bales of straw in plain sight for half of the year. "Can't you do something to 'pretty up' that garden a little?" she asked, and that was when inspiration hit. I promised to try some flowers in the sides, and see how they'd do. Within a month I had proof that they would grow well tucked into the sides of the bales and they looked great. This "skirt" of flowers planted around the sides of the bales can really add some color and beauty to the garden. Any number of different annuals will grow well and look good. You might try planting impatiens, petunias, marigolds, vinca or salvia. Select shorter varieties so that you don't end up shading the top of the bales with the annual flowers.

Add some cutting flowers to your Straw Bale Gardens and you'll thank yourself all summer long.

Fresh flowers on your table

In addition to planting annual flowers in the sides of the bales, some gardeners might venture to use their straw bales specifically to grow flowers for cutting and display inside the home. Nothing is more beautiful than a vase of fresh flowers, and nothing is more satisfying than having grown them yourself. I like to bring a nice bouquet of flowers from my garden whenever we visit friends throughout summer. You might try growing asters, celosia, cosmos, rudbekia, scabiosa, statice, sunflowers or zinnias in your bales, because all grow very well in straw bales. Harvest the blooms and fill a favorite vase for an indoor arrangement of fresh flowers every few days. You'll be amazed at how many flowers you can pack on top of one or two bales. Once the blooms are cut, you can remove the rest of the stalk to make room for other flowers coming quickly behind.

Summer bulbs the easy way

Plant summer bulbs in the bales so that after you harvest the beautiful blooms you can simply let the bulbs finish in the bale. Let the remaining leaves of the plant continue to grow and replenish the bulb, and then wither at season's end. When the bale is cut open in the fall, the bulbs can be easily harvested, without even lifting a shovel. Divide them, and store over winter for planting again the following spring. Gladiolus, dahlias, crocosmia, caladium, lily, calla and butterfly ginger are all beautiful bulbs that grow quickly, display well as cut-flowers and do well in a Straw Bale Garden.

Tip

FRESH FLOWER SUPER JUICE

Make cut flowers last up to three times as long by re-cutting the stems under warm water before arranging them. Mix one cup of 7-Up with one cup hot water and 3/4 teaspoon household bleach. Use this mixture in all of your vases from now on and your cut flowers will last much longer. Rinse out the vase every two or three days, never going four days, and always re-cut the stems by ½ inch before putting them back into fresh water mixture. The bleach will keep the vase water from emitting that nasty smell that vase water always has after a couple of days with flowers immersed into it. Your cut flowers will now last much longer than they ever have in the past.

Plant spacing chart for bales

NR means Not Recommended to plant in straw bales.

PLANT	INCHES APART	PLANTS PER BALE	CROPS/ SEASON
Arugula	2	60	3
Asparagus	15 - 18	NR	1
Beans, lima	4 - 6	30	1
Beans, pole	6 - 12	16	1
Beans, bush	4 - 6	30	1
Beets	2 - 4	48	2+
Broccoli	12 - 18	5	2
Brussels sprouts	15 - 18	4	1
Cabbage	15 - 18	4	2
Cabbage, Chinese	10 - 12	8	2+
Carrots	2 - 3	48	2
Cauliflower	15 - 18	4	2
Chili peppers	12-14	4	1
Corn salad	4-6	30	2
Chard, Swiss	6 - 9	12	2+
Collards	12 - 15	5	2+
Cucumber	12 - 18	4	1
Chard, Swiss	6 - 9	12	2+
Collards	12 - 15	5	2+
Endive	15 - 18	4	3+
Eggplant	18 - 24	3	1
Green onion	2	60	3+
Kale	15 - 18	4	2

PLANT	INCHES APART	PLANTS PER BALE	CROPS/ SEASON
Kohlrabi	6 - 9	12	1
Leeks	3 - 6	30	1
Lettuce, head	10 - 12	8	2
Lettuce, leaf	4 - 6	30	4+
Melons	18 - 24	3	1
Mustard	6 - 9	20	3
Okra	12 - 18	5	1
Onion	2 - 4	48 - 60	1
Peas	2 - 4	44	2
Peppers	12 - 15	4	1
Potatoes	10 - 12	3	1
Pumpkins	24 - 36	2	1
Radishes	2 - 3	60	3
Rutabaga	6 - 9	12	1
Sweet potato	12 - 14	4	1
Spinach	4 - 6	30	3
Squash, summer	18 - 24	3	1
Squash, winter	24 - 36	2	1
Sweet corn	15 - 18	NR	1
Tomatoes	18 - 24	2	1
Turnip	4 - 6	30	2
Water cress	2	60	2
Zucchini	18	3	1

STRAW BALE *Greenhouse*

ONE OF THE GREATEST BENEFITS of this Straw Bale Garden system is that it can give you a head start of two weeks or more on the growing season. The internal heat created by the decomposing straw is a big part of this, but to truly take advantage of the opportunity be sure to add the "greenhouse" element I've developed for a standard SBG layout. The best time to build your retractable greenhouse cover is right after you finish planting.

Use a 2- to 3-mil-thick ("mil" stands for 1/1000 of an inch, not millimeter—don't get confused) clear polyethylene sheet to make your greenhouse cover. Pull the sheeting between the two wires that are strung between the posts at the 10" height above the bales. The poly cover will hold in the heat being generated by the "cooking" bale, and keep the new transplants and seedlings warm and toasty. While the nighttime temperatures and even some daytime temperatures can be damaging to tender plants put out too early, it is virtually impossible to incur damage under the tent covers with the little compost furnace running underneath the seedbed.

The poly tent cover will hold in the heat being generated from the decomposing bale below, keeping the transplanted seedlings nice and toasty, even if the night temps drop well below freezing.

Opposite: Pull the poly covers over the top of the newly planted seed beds or tender transplants to protect them from the cool night temperatures. The cover also discourages deer, rabbits and drying wind that may damage the tender sprouts as they emerge and grow in the bales.

On a warm day when the temperature under the cover would get too hot for the seedlings, pull the poly cover to the end of the bale row and clip it around the end post. If the temperature forecast is for anything over 65° F, the covers should be pulled back. If the nighttime temps fall below 45°, then the covers should be pulled back over the bales.

Move the covers higher as plants grow

As transplants and seedlings grow, they will soon be touching the poly cover. The larger the volume of area covered by the poly tent, the greater the amount of air that has to be heated by the "cooking" bale, so keep the covers as low as possible. Move the covers up from the 10-inch wire to the 20-inch wire only when the plants are touching the covers.

Pull poly covers off on warm or sunny days

The temperature under the poly covers during the day can get very warm, especially when the sun is shining, so be prepared to slide the cover to one end and clip it behind the end post at the start of any day with a weather forecast calling for at least 65° and sun. Keep the covers off until the forecast calls for temps cooler than 45° at night and then pull the covers back over the top. Keep the covers on until the forecast calls for daytime temperatures above 65°. This system seems to work very well, and you'll be surprised at how few times you will actually have to pull the covers over or remove them in one growing season. Keep in mind that the covers are also there to protect the seedbed from any really hard rain, or from hungry wildlife looking for a salad bar.

Row cover cloth is also a great option

Row cover cloth is an alternative to the clear poly film that is worth considering, especially if the temperatures where you are located rarely get to below 30°. The poly can actually get too warm on sunny days. The row cover cloth breathes better and yet will retain much of the heat from the "cooking" bales around the plants. Row cover cloth normally comes in 6-foot width, so if you simply get enough to cover the length of your row of bales you will have plenty. It is reusable for many years, and reasonably priced, so it might be worth it to keep some around for those years when the weather warms up early and the poly covers would be too hot. I like to start early in the year, when it is very cool at night with two layers of poly at 10 and 20 inches high, then pull one off about a week into the season. Then after another week or two when day temperatures are consistently 65° and above, I switch to the row cover cloth. Depending on what you buy, some row cover cloth will let in up to 95% of the sun's rays, and yet it will keep any flying insects, wildlife and birds from snacking on your young transplants and seedlings.

Tuck in tight when it's a chilly night

If the air temperature will stay in the 30s or warmer, there is no need to tuck the greenhouse covers tightly under the bale strings. But if the forecast is to reach down into the 20s, then tuck the poly cover sides tightly under the strings, and wrap the ends snugly around the posts to prevent wind from getting up under the covers. If the strings are too tight on the bales, and you are not able to tuck the plastic

Below: If the air temperature threatens to fall into the 20s, make sure the sides and the ends of the greenhouse covers are tucked in nice and tight to keep the cold air out.

behind them, just drape the poly over the top and then tie a long piece of rope or twine all the way around the bottom of all the bales in that row and on top of the poly sides. Tie the rope nice and taut. The bales will stay cozy and warm, and your seedlings will think they are inside a comfy greenhouse, even though the temperatures outside may fall through the 20s.

For the first three to five weeks of your garden's life, the plants will be growing much of the time under these covers, where their roots are toasty warm. This gives them a big head start on the season. It is fun to compare some plants grown in your Straw Bale Garden with the same size transplant put into the soil nearby. The difference in growth will astound you, until you realize the soil will normally be 20 to 30° cooler than the planting zone of the bales. This head start on the season translates to crops that mature earlier. Earlier harvest in the fall means crops won't get caught by early fall frost before ripening. If you are ever caught unprepared by an early forecast for a hard frost, it is easy to grab the poly covers and using them sideways pull them over the entire trellis and cover the whole garden. This tenting of the whole garden will provide significant protection from frost damage, possibly giving your plants another couple of weeks of growing season to finish.

No gas, no electricity, just bacteria hard at work

A traditional greenhouse employs electric or gas heaters that are regulated by a thermostat to keep the air from falling below a set temperature. Our straw bale greenhouse requires no supplemental heat because it is very rare that the temperatures will ever get low enough to cause any problems. As the bacteria are digesting or composting the straw, they give off a great deal of heat. You may like to leave a thermometer on top of the bales under the covers, so you can check on the temperatures on occasion. It is rather common to see a reading that is 15 to 30 degrees warmer than the outside air temperatures, even on a partly sunny day.

Double the poly if the temperatures crash

If the forecast were to retreat fully to winter temperatures and drop below 20°, I would recommend adding another layer of poly film above the one at 10 inches, using the two wires at 20". This sandwich of two layers of polyethylene film will trap a layer of air in-between. Trapped dead air has an incredible insulating capacity to protect from cold temperatures, and with the bacteria heater running inside the bales your mini straw bale greenhouse will stay toasty warm.

Clear seed tray covers work well to cover the tender seedbed if the polyethylene sheeting covers are not going to be used. Make sure to use a piece of bent-over wire like a giant staple to punch through each end of the covers and into the bale to hold them in place.

Seed tray covers as another option

Once the seeds are planted, the tender seedbed will need to be protected. If the plastic sheeting described earlier is not being used, then cover each bale with two clear seed tray covers to protect the seedbed and the tender seedlings. The seed tray covers will help hold in some of the heat being generated from the conditioning bale, but will also protect the seedbed from any hazards. At this point in the early spring, hazards would include heavy rainfall, cold air or wildlife looking for a snack. Use some 30-inch lengths of wire bent over like giant staples, sticking them through the seed tray covers and into the bales to hold the covers in place. The covers are usually about 2 inches deep, so this will give your seedlings a chance to emerge and establish a little bit of root and a couple of leaves before the seed tray covers will need to be pulled off. If you are using the soaker hose already buried right in the seedbed to water, then there will be no need to remove the covers to water. Leave them in place unless it gets above 70°, in which case they will need to be pulled off or the seedlings can get too hot.

When the covers come off, the netting goes on

Once the poly covers (or the row cover cloth) can come off for the summer, it is a good idea to replace the cover with bird netting. Bird netting is by definition meant to keep birds from damaging the garden, but it does a good job of keeping rabbits and deer from doing major damage as well. Normally I like to drape the netting over top of the top wood rail on the trellis and let it fall down to the ground on both sides. Netting, much like polyethylene, comes in many different sizes, but I would recommend the 14-foot width, and whatever length your garden calls for. I like the ¾-inch mesh; it works best for birds and rabbits, and keeps the deer away as well.

Growing YOUR STRAW BALE GARDEN

ALMOST EVERY BOOK I have ever read on vegetable gardening dedicates a big chunk of space to dealing with weeds. You should pull them, hoe them, spray them, cover them up, cut them off or kill them with any method you can devise. My Grandma Josephine's retort whenever her grandkids would complain about having to weed the garden was always, "Well, if it weren't for the weeds, everyone would be a gardener!" If you have purchased clean straw bales, used sterile potting mix for the seedbed on top of the bales and covered the space between rows with a weed barrier, this will be your first summer of vegetable gardening without weeds. That said, if you do happen to get a couple of weed seeds that blow in from the neighbor's garden, you should deal with them right away—allow yourself 30 seconds, per bale, per season, and that should cover any possible weeding you might need to do. That's it. We are done talking about weeds now, as they are just not of any concern with a Straw Bale Garden. Now there's no excuse: Everyone should have a garden, at least according to my Grandma Josephine.

Opposite: Once your plants are well-rooted and established, caring for your Straw Bale Garden is not that different from a soil-based garden: with one exception—No Weeding!

Dear Joel: Just a note to thank you for the information you sent on how to grow a Straw Bale Garden. I read your no weeds statement with a cynical chuckle, and my husband only rolled his eyes. Now I must confess to you that I had nary five weeds all summer in my whole garden. You were almost telling the truth! Thanks again.
—Judith

In the midst of fertilizing his Straw Bale Garden with a hose end applicator, this young man is learning a new way of gardening as part of his 4-H project.

Monthly fertilizer applications will keep everything green

An application of a liquid or soluble fertilizer is recommended every few weeks throughout the growing season. Don't apply any fertilizer to very small seedlings, however. Instead, wait until the seedlings have grown their third leaf pair, and then they can be safely fertilized. Organic gardeners should use an organic foliar fertilizer, like fish emulsion, kelp emulsion or similar. On my organic bales I use a fish emulsion, which smells bad but works great. If using traditional refined foliar fertilizer, I like the Miracle Gro® soluble fertilizer. It is well balanced and liquefies easily. The refined fertilizer is less expensive, but in the interest of my organic studies, I spend the extra money to keep those bales 100% organic.

When novice gardeners would visit her garden they often would ask my Grandma Josephine, "How can we tell when we should water our garden?" She would look at them, point her finger in the air and say, "Use this. God gave everybody one, it's your built-in moisture checker." Her advice still holds true with a Straw Bale Garden. If your garden feels dry when you push your finger into the bale, it probably needs a drink. I recommend that you water early in the day; this allows all the leaves to dry completely, long before the sun sets. Especially during the warm sultry nights of summer, having wet leaves overnight can give bacteria, mold, fungus and other pathogens lots of time to grow and spread in the warm water on the leaf. When watering your garden by hand, keep the spray nozzle underneath the canopy of the plants and water only the roots. The soaker hose is still the easiest and most efficient way to water a Straw Bale Garden. Water applied to the surface of a bale through a soaker hose will work its way over to even the edges of the bale.

Hi Joel. I've been doing a small straw bale garden for my tomatoes, peppers and squash since 2008. I am on the NC coast and the bales have worked great. For the last couple of summers, when we have had months of drought . . . the bales stayed moist and required very little water. I watered weekly using a gallon of water per bale during that time (I actually used my AC condensate).
I can't say enough good about the process, it's so easy and practically takes care of itself! Thanks again for the info on Straw Bale Gardening.
—Sandy

Straw Bale Gardening = fewer pests = fewer pesticides

Just about everyone who is serious about gardening tries to avoid using harmful chemicals to kill bugs and weeds—or to solve any other problems for that matter. This is especially true when the plan includes eventually eating the vegetables, or feeding them to your loved ones. Straw Bale Gardening is not going to solve every insect problem that happens in gardens, but keep in mind that many traditional problems with insects and weeds come specifically from using the same soil year after year in a traditional soil garden. Pick up any good book written by a traditional gardening expert, and it will emphasize the importance of crop rotations, thus acknowledging this issue and in a small way attempting to avoid the accumulation of problems. When Straw Bale Gardeners start each spring with a fresh bale of straw, we are actually creating our own planting mix, without ANY of these lingering problems. None of the previous year's insects, diseases, viruses, funguses, or weed seeds are present in this newly generated planting mix inside the bales. This is key to avoiding many of these most difficult and most common problems that discourage so many gardeners.

A GREAT WAY to tell if your garden needs water by simply looking out your kitchen window is to plant a couple of indicator plants in the garden. I like to use impatiens, tall red ones work well so I can see the flowers from a distance. Impatiens have shallow roots, and they tend to get droopy and they wilt easily if the roots get dry, but then they perk right back up once they get a drink. A quick look at the indicator plants in the garden will help determine if things are getting dry, just look for perky or wilted impatiens from inside the house.

Designing a garden so that it is less attractive to insects like these Japanese beetles is a great way to help keep them at bay.

Stay alert for bugs and those ugly slugs

I won't go so far as to tell you that you are out of the woods when it comes to battling some of nature's champion garden pests just because you have become a Straw Bale Gardener. I do think it is important to try to understand a few things from the perspective of a pest. If you know what the pest is looking for, often you can design your garden in a way to make it less pest friendly, thereby avoiding many common problems. Insects are normally looking for only two things: food and shelter. The shelter is usually for reproduction or egg-laying purposes. Finding a leaf, or a root or a stem that is food is instinctual for most insects. A cabbage caterpillar is looking for a cabbage leaf to eat, and Mother Nature hasn't instilled in the caterpillar the instinct to look on top of a bale of straw. Rather, instinct tells it to crawl along the soil and look around for a cabbage stem to climb. Cabbage root fly maggots are another example: They will instinctively lay eggs on the soil around the stem of the cabbage, the maggots hatch and eat the roots below. With the cabbage planted in a straw bale, there isn't soil around the stem of the cabbage transplants, so when they lay eggs on the surface of straw the eggs will dry up before they can hatch.

One of the best ways to solve pest problems is to simply pluck the critters off the leaves and dispose of them. That sounds like a simple solution, and it is, but it works. Spend ten minutes, especially in the morning, plucking any slugs, caterpillars, beetles, etc., from the leaves. Take an extra careful look at the underside of leaves. Diligence here will usually keep your garden pests at bay. It doesn't make sense to use a spray bottle of insecticidal soap, which only kills the bugs you actually hit with the spray, when you could just grab and bag the bugs instead.

Keeping the plants spaced properly in a garden is a very important element of pest control, because it allows for plentiful airflow in and around leaves and allows the plants to dance around in the wind. This airflow keeps moisture off the leaves, but it also builds stem strength from the constant movement, which contributes to making plants less desirable to insects.

In a Straw Bale Garden, the plants are 20 to 24 inches up off the ground to start with, which certainly allows better airflow. Keeping the rows of bales far enough apart that one row doesn't shade another or block the wind from another row is also important. Overcrowding a garden is detrimental when it comes to insects. Avoid overplanting, and remember to thin seedlings once they have germinated to avoid future pest problems.

Pesticides have a place in agriculture and even in lawns and some gardens, but diligent gardeners can solve most problems without them.

"NO DEER ALLOWED"

Hang a few signs like this around your garden and you won't have to worry about wildlife in your garden, because you're in dreamland, where animals can read! Rabbits, raccoons, squirrels, woodchucks, large birds, deer and the neighbor's dog are all pesky critters that, in reality, can destroy a newly planted garden in only minutes. Over the years a thousand homespun ideas and natural deterrents have been developed, many that may work sometimes, but none of which work all the time. A fence may be a deterrent, but a whitetail deer can clear an 8-foot fence without much difficulty, and a rabbit or a woodchuck can dig under a fence in about 60 seconds, so that may not be an option either.

Critters are looking for food or shelter, so keep in mind they are not going after your garden just to make you go berserk, but only because Mother Nature is telling them to look there for a buffet lunch. Defending your garden means starting very early before the problem animal has ever found the buffet and learned to come back daily for a snack. Keeping them away initially can make return visits much less likely. I am by my nature rather skeptical and I don't fall for gimmicks. I actually pride myself on my ability to sniff out the scam in everything, so mind you the suggestion I am making here isn't offered lightly, but with a great deal of personal research. The invention by some smart Canadian entrepreneur of the motion-sensitive ScareCrow® sprinkler is nothing less than genius. It is not an inexpensive solution in that it cost four times what a regular sprinkler costs, but they are extremely simple to use, very effective, and seem to last for many years. Think back to a time when you were walking up to a neighbor's home after dark, and just as you got near the front step, BAMMO all the flood lights on the garage came on, and you nearly swallowed your tongue! This is the same basic motion-sensing technology that these sprinklers use. You'll hook the ScareCrow up to a garden hose with the water on, and install a single 9-volt battery in the unit. Anything that moves, day or night, for 35 feet in front of that sprinkler gets blasted with water in a three-second burst with a loud hissing sound as well. After this blast the sprinkler turns off, waits a few seconds and the sensors come on again, ready to blast another invader. It is amazing how smart animals are. They learn within a very short time that getting blasted by cold water in the middle of the night isn't worth it, and the problem critters will not enter the area. I can tell you that the first time I forgot that sprinkler was there, I was blasted with cold water, my heart skipped three beats while I caught my breath, and my wife nearly died just from laughing as she watched out the window. I haven't forgotten it was there ever since!

I don't make many specific product endorsements, but I have found that the ScareCrow motion-activated sprinklers (See Resources, page 172) are an effective and humane way to keep small animal pests out of your garden. Just remember to turn it off before you head out in your pajamas to pick some thyme for your omelet.

Turns out, I accidentally bought hay bales, whoops

If it turns out that you are growing a Chia Pet in your garden, as the seeds in the hay bales that you thought were straw bales have now sprouted, don't worry. I have a quick and easy solution. Mix ½ gallon of white vinegar with a squirt of dish soap, and pour it into a cake pan or a paint tray. Now rustle up that old sponge mop from the storage closet—you know, the one where you pull the handle down to squeeze out any extra liquid. Mop this solution of vinegar onto the sprouts. Your garden may smell like salad dressing for the next day, but the solution is very safe for you and your pets. The sprouts will be dead in 24 hours, with no lingering toxicity from the vinegar.

If you already have plants in the bales, be very careful to not get the solution on the plants you want to keep. The vinegar is non-selective and will kill any plant it touches. To apply the vinegar solution in between plants, try slipping on a rubber glove (dishwashing glove works great) and then put on a cotton or cloth glove over the top. Dip your fingers into the vinegar and squeeze out any excess. Now whatever you touch with that glove will soon be history. Rinse and dry the "glove of death" before using it again for gardening.

The bale on the left turned out to be canary grass hay, while the bale on the right is oat straw. The sprouts are essentially harmless and will dry up after a couple of weeks, but can also be cut off with a knife or mopped with vinegar.

My bales are getting a little tipsy

If one or more of your bales begins to tip a little bit sideways as it cooks and your plants grow, it's a fair bet that the bale was loose and not well compacted. This may seem like a time to panic, but the fix is very simple. Push a long board, like a 2 x 6 or a 2 x 8, up against the side of the bale tightly enough to push it upright. Then, pound a little wooden stake in next to the board to hold it in place. In a couple of weeks you can even remove the board and the bale will usually stay upright after that.

This tipping problem can also be caused by too much water, so dial back the water just a little if this starts happening in your garden. I visited a Straw Bale Garden where more than half of the bales had tipped over sideways, but it was still growing just fine. The plants hardly seemed to notice, they just turned upward again, and kept right on growing. I don't recommend it, but it seems overall it had little effect on the garden's performance.

Eventually, every straw bale will fall apart. Normally this does not happen until well after the growing season is concluded. But sometimes (usually because the bale was not compressed tightly enough) bales disintegrate prematurely. If your bale is starting to come undone, simply buttress it with a stake and a wide board on the side to which it is leaning—or on both sides in more extreme cases.

Stacking bales in the garden

Years ago, when I first started Straw Bale Gardening, I actually tried stacking bales on top of one another. It didn't work well at all. About halfway through the year I already had posts pounded in every which way around the bales to try to keep the top bale from falling off the bottom bale. After that experiment I told everyone that stacking bales just didn't work very well. Then one day, I received a note and some pictures from a Straw Bale Gardener named J. J. Lawson from Illinois who proved my advice on this was a bit premature. She had grown a very successful garden and had stacked the bales up to do it. She simply laid the first layer down lengthwise, and then turned the second layer the other direction. Her garden seemed to have two tiers for planting, and grew wonderfully as documented in her photos. I was wrong about stacking bales, she was right and she proved it actually works rather well. If you are extremely averse to bending over at all you might try her method. Keep in mind that if you put a tomato plant up there, you'll need a step ladder when it comes time to pick tomatoes. It just goes to show, there are always better ideas and innovations to old ideas that can make things easier.

This photo is part of a series a Straw Bale Gardener sent to me to demonstrate that double stacking bales is certainly possible. Note the bottom bales are turned lengthwise and the top one is turned sideways, making a tiered garden.

Growing the perfect tomatoes starts with the perfect tomato tower. This is one you can build for $5 in a few minutes, and it will last forever.

TOMATO TOWERS THAT LAST FOREVER AND COST $5

Growing the perfect tomato starts with the perfect tomato cage. Build your own for less than $5 each. All you need is a bolt cutter, some zip ties, and a roll of concrete reinforcing wire from the home center or lumber yard. Just like the name says, this wire grid is made to be buried in concrete for reinforcing concrete so it doesn't easily crack. The wire is inexpensive and measures 5 feet wide by any length you desire. Use the bolt cutter to cut off a 6- or 7-foot section, depending on how tall you want the cages to be. Roll the wire panel up in the opposite direction from the way it was unrolled. When the sides come together use the zip ties to fasten them. This makes a tall, 2-foot diameter cylindrical cage that is absolutely perfect for growing tomatoes and for many other climbing plants.

The ends, where you cut the wire to length, will be sticking down on the bottom like little steel fingers. Push them down into the straw bale and the cage will be fixed in place for the season. Reinforce the cage with a fence post if you are using it on top of a straw bale, or else it can get very topheavy and may fall over. You can also stick with the concrete theme and use a length of rebar or two to stake the cage.

The openings in the wire panels are big (usually 6 x 6 inches), so reaching in to harvest tomatoes inside the cage is really easy. At the end of the season, if storage space is a problem, simply cut the zip ties off, and flatten out the panels in your garden. The panels will rust over the years, but mine are still going strong after 15 years. I used to make these and sell them at the farmers market when I was younger. People loved them, and I am sure most are still using them all these many years later.

Above: Harvesting begins not long after planting in the spring, with leafy greens ready to cut within three or four weeks of seeding. Replanting once a crop has been harvested is a key to maximizing the use of the bales in your garden.

Left: Regularly prune the flowers off basil and other leafy herbs to encourage more foliage growth.

SBGs AND WATER

THERE IS MORE THAN ONE WAY TO WATER a Straw Bale Garden. In many parts of the world water is a scarce resource. Although I'm lucky enough to live in an area where water supply isn't really an issue, I realize this only means that it isn't an issue yet. Conserving water use is important, and I set out a few years ago to try some methods of watering that were more precise and thus more conservative than my original "soaker hose down the middle" technique. I have transitioned most of my Straw Bale Gardens today to a dripper system. The initial investment was about $100, and that allows me to cover 24 bales with precision applicators that emit a specific amount of GPH (gallons per hour) to each plant. I set up the emitters with the idea that some plants use much more water than others, and this allows me to adjust the individual emitters to slow the water to some plants and increase the flow to others, thus saving water. I can water the whole garden for the same length of time and get different volumes of water on each individual plant.

I still believe using a hose end timer is essential. The effort to water everything by hand is admirable, but we are only human, and the likelihood that you may forget to turn the water on or to turn the hose off a few times during the year can have dire consequences. Also remember to always use a splitter right off of your water spigot;

Opposite: A drip system with regularly spaced emitters is easier to control than a plain old soaker hose, but it costs more and takes more time to set up. The drip system will last many years without needing replacement, unlike the soaker hoses which often start to spring leaks after a year or two.

Space the emitters every 12" or so along the main supply line. Customize the tubing length to each emitter so you can adjust its position to put water exactly where each plant is rooting into the bale.

Right: If you are using soaker hoses to water your bales, you may want to double the hose to increase watering speed, and to water in a wider distribution pattern.

A small pond pump can be set into your rain barrel to deliver water to your SBG via a hose.

this prevents someone from unhooking your hose to use the faucet for a second and then forgetting to hook it back up.

Rain barrels or collection tanks are common sources of water for many gardeners, and that makes using a dripper system impossible to use . . . or does it? It turns out that a simple lamp timer and an electric pond pump work very well together to take water from a rain barrel and make a dripper system work just fine. Look for a pond pump that pumps at least 15 feet high (this is how they are rated), which should create enough pressure to water up to 30 bales very easily in one zone. The digital lamp timer can be programmed just like a hose end timer, so it comes on at a specific time of day for a specified amount of time. Try to apply about one or two gallons of water per bale per application. Larger amounts will usually run right through the bale and be wasted. For example, if you have 10 bales,

RECYCLING YOUR WATER

Recycling water used in a straw bale garden is really pretty easy. Start by laying down a 5-foot-wide length of 6 mil (a measurement for plastic, and does not mean millimeters) black plastic sheeting. Stretch it the length of your planned row of bales. Lay some old boards down along the edges of the plastic and staple the plastic to the boards. Now roll the boards underneath the plastic from both edges to create a plastic trough about 2 feet wide, so the bales will easily sit on top of the plastic trough you've created. Depending on the slope of your garden, the water will run to one end or the other. On the lower end of the trough, dig a hole in the ground big enough to fit a 5-gallon bucket so the lip of the bucket is underneath the level of the plastic trough. Every time you water your straw bales, excess water will run through the bales, down the plastic trough and into the bucket. Use a pond pump to automate the recirculation process or just lift the bucket out by hand, dump it on the bales and quickly put it back into the collection hole. It is amazing how little water is wasted when implementing this system. It is inexpensive, costing less than 25 cents per bale to buy the plastic at any home store.

The components of water recycling system include black plastic sheeting, a 5-gallon bucket buried in a hole and a recirculating pond pump with hose.

apply 10 to 20 gallons each time you water. Most folks have about 2 gallons per minute of water coming out of a garden hose, so that means you need about 30 seconds to 1 minute per bale per application. In the case of a ten-bale garden that means 5 to 10 minutes will do the trick. Watering every two or three days will probably be adequate early in the spring and in the late fall, but during the heat of summer you may want to water your garden twice a day, applying one or two gallons to each bale every time. Consistent moisture is essential to healthy and productive vegetable plants. Watch your plants carefully and look for any leaf wilting; this will tell you they need water more often.

Tip

I heard from one Straw Bale Gardener who used only the condensate from her air conditioning unit to water her three-bale garden. This alone provided plenty of water all summer long, so it may surprise you how little water it actually takes to maintain a healthy and productive Straw Bale Garden.

Harvest TIME

I AM NOT SURE WHY this section about harvest comes at the end of the book, since harvesting actually starts within three weeks of the planting date, in many cases anyway. Planting days will come again almost weekly once harvest begins, and the whole summer will be filled with a little harvesting and a little planting every week for most of the summer. Keeping a garden busy growing new seeds once an initial crop is harvested is a key to maximizing the space we have available for production. Virtually any crop that matures within 60 days can be planted at least twice per year even in the more northern climates. Planting in rotation, so that no surface area on the bales is left idle and thus wasted for any of the growing season will maximize the use of the bales in your garden.

Harvesting daily helps keep your garden healthy

Most vegetable gardens begin producing leafy salad greens, radish, spinach, beets, okra and zucchini within just 30 days of planting. Harvest the radish, beets and okra, and get another crop planted on the heels of the first. Cut the leafy greens, spinach and collards, and let them regenerate another leaf. When the second leaf grows back just pull the whole plant out by the roots for the second harvest, and replant. A cucumber can grow 5 inches in just 24 hours during prime season, so keep an eye out for ripe produce daily. Continue harvesting daily as crops are ready, because over-ripe vegetables, left unpicked, are an invitation to insects and other problems.

Opposite: Harvest time happens all season long, but it's in the late summer and early fall when the showcase crops, like these savoy cabbages, are ready for picking.

Freshness measured in hours, not days or weeks

In some cases, vegetables begin to deteriorate in quality very quickly, and should be eaten within hours of harvest, rather than waiting days or weeks. A great example of this is sweet corn (even though this is not a great SBG crop). If you have never tasted fresh corn, and I mean corn that was just pulled out of the field husked immediately and plunged for three minutes into boiling water, then you don't really know what truly fresh corn tastes like. It is spectacular! Fresh corn isn't fresh if it was harvested this morning or yesterday or a week ago. It begins to lose flavor and freshness within an hour or two of being harvested. Wait until the water is boiling, then run to the garden and harvest the corn!

Pulling a fresh radish as big as a lollipop from the garden and washing it off quickly under a faucet, and eating it while standing in the garden, is an experience nobody will ever forget doing as a child. It was only the beginning for me—soon it was carrots, beans and peas, strawberries, raspberries and cucumbers. It was something that I looked forward to every day as a kid, working in the garden with my Grandma Josephine. "Save some for dinner" was her reliable advice. There is nothing better than walking to the garden and returning 15 minutes later with a full spread of fresh vegetables for you and your family to enjoy for lunch and dinner.

Basil: the king of the herbs

When your basil is looking fantastic mid-season, of course it is nearly impossible to use it all at once. Here is a tip I've learned: Every time you prune, or harvest from this beautiful big basil plant, remove the stems and wash the leaves in a cold water bath. Roll up a handful of leaves and use a scissors to cut them up into a pile of aromatic deliciousness. Stuff a pinch of leaves into the bottom of every empty hole in an empty ice cube tray. Fill each cube with good olive oil, make sure no basil is sticking up, and make sure to work quickly so the shredded basil doesn't dry out. Freeze the trays in your freezer at least overnight. Pop the cubes into a plastic zip lock bag and put them immediately back into the freezer. The olive oil will help to maintain the bright green color of the fresh basil. When winter arrives, every time a recipe calls for fresh basil, use one cube for each tablespoon the recipe requires. So easy, so delicious, and very inexpensive. I have been forced to buy one of the small plastic packs of fresh basil for a recipe now and again in the middle of winter. I realize only then, that for half of the summer I am actually a

PLEASE . . . PLEASE TAKE A FEW MORE TOMATOES, WON'T YOU?

Free Tomatoes! Like clockwork every August, the offices around town are filled with surplus tomatoes, with a paper sign proclaiming "free tomatoes." Big Boys, Big Girls, Beef this, Beef that, and by this time of year so many gardeners who planted a dozen of the BIG hybrid varieties that produce 50 to 75 pounds of tomatoes per plant, are now "tomato drunk." Their eyes bloodshot from eating twelve tomatoes every day for the previous five weeks, they turn to coworkers, friends and relatives to help them consume this vast surplus of red manna.

All the really good tomatoes, the Sutton Brandywine, African Queen, Old Ivory Egg and Aunt Gerdie's Gold have been eaten, devoured like candy the morning after Halloween. When they ripen, they must be eaten quickly, for they won't keep more than two or three days, so you'll have to grow these yourself if you ever want a taste. Their very thin skin is one reason they don't store well and can't be transported far. Store-bought tomatoes are often picked green and then exposed to ethylene gas to ripen them as they are delivered to the store shelves. Sometimes they taste like they were exposed to methane gas if you ask me, and not very good at all. These heirloom varieties are the cream, the cherries on top, and the reason Mother Nature is held in such esteem. The best thing you'll ever taste. I would argue that may be true, especially after a cold winter having endured six months of ketchup-flavored tennis balls painted red at the store.

millionaire with the amount of fresh basil I have growing around my gardens. I have so much that often before we have company for a night outside on the patio, I will grab an entire bush, and take the lawn mower over the top of it, mulching it into the lawn. It smells delicious for about two or three days, and everyone wonders why it always smells so great in my backyard. Now I've given away my secret. The problem is that six months later, in the middle of winter, everyone who doesn't have a heated greenhouse is at the mercy of the basil growers that do. This frozen cube method also works for rosemary, chives, lemon balm, mint and tarragon.

A favorite of many, basil is one of the most popular herbs, but it doesn't store well, and tends to turn black quickly, losing its fresh taste and color.

Potatoes without digging

Potatoes should be planted very deep inside the bale, around 10 to 12 inches. The stem will find its way to the surface, and the long stem will produce lots of potatoes inside the bale. Potatoes are part of the stem, not the root, so long stems produce more potatoes. It is recommended to plant three seed potatoes per bale with another early season crop on the surface of the bale, like lettuce or radish. In the early fall when the vine flowers, the potatoes are likely ready. When the vine starts to wither, simply cut the strings of the bale; the bale will spill open and the potatoes will be easy picking with no digging. No fork or shovel damage, either, in the potatoes that are gathered for storage. Unblemished potatoes do store well in a cool, dark, dry area; wrap them in newspaper or brown paper as this extends their storage life as well.

Potatoes will develop inside the bale, and by cutting the strings and knocking the bale over, harvesting the potatoes couldn't be easier. Simply pick them up. They will be pretty clean, unlike muddy potatoes I used to dig up in Grandma's garden.

You'll want to employ several different strategies for preserving your SBG produce, from canning to drying to pickling to freezing and more.

"Putting up" vegetables

I would recommend at the same time you are planning the details about what you'll plant in your garden that you take time to learn how to "put up" the excess of any of those vegetables you are planting. Learning the basics about how to properly freeze, pickle, can, dry, hang, sand pack, bag and preserve those vegetables coming out of your garden can keep your supply of garden vegetables coming year-round. Most methods are not difficult, and the difference in taste from the store-bought vegetables is well worth the time and effort it takes, not to mention the savings. Imagine bringing jars of your homemade sweet pepper jelly to all of your friends at holiday time, with a note that says "Homegrown with love in my Straw Bale Garden." Maybe with a copy of this book tucked in the gift basket!

Shouldn't it be called jarring not canning . . .

"Canning" vegetables is actually a process where the vegetables are put into jars with liquid around them, and a rubber sealed metal lid is fitted on top. The jars are lowered into a boiling water bath, which heats the jars and contents, killing any bacteria that may exist inside the jars. The lids are pressure sealed onto the now sterile jars and will normally store for years in these jars without going bad. This method of preservation has lost much of its appeal as we have flash-frozen bags of every fruit and vegetable crop known to man available 365 days a year at your nearest grocery store.

Below: When canning, you may choose to keep your produce as close to its natural state as possible so you have many options for using it, or you may choose to can big batches of your favorite soup, sauce, chutney or salsa.

Freezing vegetables involves science

Don't be fooled by the idea that simply freezing what cannot be used immediately is a good option for every vegetable. Don't assume that you can simply thaw out those veggies later for a great dinner in January. It will not work for many crops, and the vegetables or fruit will end up as mush when you thaw them. Why can the frozen vegetables from the store be so good, while some frozen vegetables from home can be so horrible? It all has to do with the freezer used to freeze them and whether or not they were blanched prior to freezing. Flash-freezing at very cold temperatures like -40°F allows the water molecules inside and around the vegetables to be instantly frozen and are not given time to adhere to one another.

Clarence Birdseye is credited with inventing in 1924 the quick freezing method which produces the type of frozen foods that we know today. Using a home freezer causes the freezing process to happen but much more slowly, giving the water molecules time to adhere to one another and expand as they freeze. Once thawed, the cells in the vegetables are blown apart and thus everything turns to mush, so avoid the temptation to freeze all of your garden's produce. The only exceptions are those things that are okay to be mushy or that have fairly low water content.

Tip

STORING FROZEN PRODUCE

Rinse out some gallon milk jugs, fill them with clean water and tuck them into your chest freezer around your produce. Do this after the produce is frozen, though, or have them frozen solid when the produce hits the frigid air. The jugs of ice allow your freezer to function more efficiently because they eliminate the air pockets around the food.

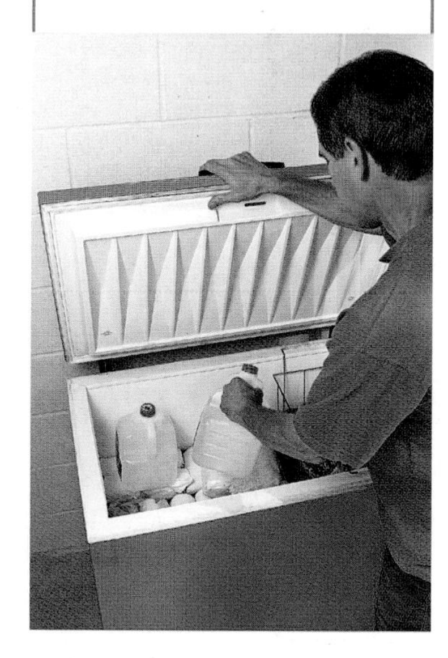

Some things just don't freeze well

Most vegetables and fruits with high water content do not freeze well and will not be appetizing when thawed. Foods from the garden that should never be frozen include celery, radishes, melons, lettuce and cucumbers.

Some vegetables do freeze well

Other vegetables do freeze very well, but generally the best technique is to blanch them, move them immediately to an ice bath, then dry them quickly (times will vary so look up recommendations online) and pack to freeze, putting a small quantity at a time into a COLD freezer, one that maintains 0°F. This assures fast freezing, which keeps them more crisp when thawed. You are simply copying some of Clarence's best technique.

Blanch and freeze asparagus, beans, lima beans, snap beans, beets, black-eyed peas, broccoli, Brussels sprouts, cabbage, carrots, cauliflower, corn on the cob, whole kernel corn, creamed-style corn, eggplant, mushrooms, onions, peas, green peppers, bell peppers, chili peppers, potatoes, pumpkins, rutabaga, squash, sweet potatoes and turnips.

WHAT REMAINS IS *Gold*

GOLD? YES, GOLD, but not the precious metal, rather the perfect compost. Gardeners' "black gold" is exactly what remains after the harvest is complete. The valuable compost left behind has many uses and can solve problems anywhere in your yard or garden.

To compost your bales, first remove any nylon strings, wood stakes, wire, and soaker hoses that made up the Straw Bale Garden. Pile up all the remaining straw/compost, and allow it to finish composting until the following spring (putting it into a pile accelerates the composting action). Toss a few more handfuls of the refined lawn fertilizer or some organic nitrogen source on top of the pile. Turn the pile every two or three weeks, and sprinkle the pile with water if it doesn't rain. I recommend keeping the straw compost separated from any regular compost pile you may already use. Keeping additional organic material out of this straw bale compost pile will maintain the consistency in particle structure and fertility, while maintaining its weed-free pedigree. The pile will finish decomposing any remaining straw particles over the winter months, and in the spring the resulting compost will AMAZE you. Use this compost to fill all of your containers, pots and window boxes, and you'll observe how much flowers love this growing medium. It will be very fertile, well drained, but still will hold moisture well. The compost will have very few or no weed seeds in the mix, but best of all it's free!

Opposite: A simple compost bin positioned near your Straw Bale Garden can be filled with organic plant waste and, at the end of the season, the remains of your straw bales. If you have another garden that uses compost you might choose not to blend the weed-free composted straw with the regular waste, however. You won't need the compost for next year's SBG, but you'll find dozens of uses around your lawn and yard for this "black gold."

A straw bale at the end of the growing season is a little grayer and looser from a spring and summer of hard work. Pile your spent straw bales together to finish composting more efficiently.

You will be able to use straw bale compost to enhance or modify existing soil where you currently grow annual flowers, perennials or other vegetables. If you are planting trees or shrubs, use 50% of the compost mixed with 50% of the virgin soil from the planting hole to give them a big head start. If your existing soils are generally heavy, clay-based, poorly drained soils, try mixing 5 inches of this compost into the top 5 inches of the existing soil to amend its structure and vastly improve drainage capacity. If your existing soils are composed of a high percentage of sand, this compost can also solve many of the problems that sandy soils foster. Cover the virgin soil with 5 inches of compost and dig it into the top 5 inches of topsoil. The resulting mix will contain enough organic matter to hold moisture and provide fertility that will sustain plant growth without daily watering and weekly fertilizing. If you have done a scrupulously careful job of segregating and composting your bales, the result can even be used to create the seedbed on top of next year's Straw Bale Garden instead of buying bagged planting mix.

Every garden needs one, or two, or even three

A good compost bin has a few characteristics that make it functional and practical. It should be easy to access for loading, so the sides cannot all be permanent. It should also be easy to access when you need to turn the pile, which means it needs a door that can be opened up all the way to the ground even when the bin is full. It needs to be unrestrictive of airflow, so air can easily get in to all sides and keep the pile aerated. It should be attractive, or at least not ugly, because nobody wants an eyesore sitting on their property all year. Finally, it should be inexpensive and easy to construct. The bins I build cost under $10, and take less than ten minutes to build. You need the following materials:

- Five short metal fence posts. The ones I use are 5 feet tall with metal fence grab tabs that point upwards on one side of the post. These are $1 each.
- An 8- to 10-foot length of 4-foot tall open wire fence. Any type works fine, but I like the welded 4 × 2-inch panel style. The cost should be $3 max for 8 feet, but you may need to buy a whole roll, and share.
- Ten pieces of 1 × 4 or 1 × 6 "value lumber" approximately 3 to 5 feet long. Cost is $.20 each, or you can pull them off of any old pallet you find lying around for free.

Joel, In all my 85 years I've just never seen such a wonderful idea. I stopped gardening a few years ago when my husband passed away, and I missed our garden so much. My daughter found your information about growing in straw bales, and helped me get two bales started last spring. I grew the best tomatoes I ever remember growing. Isn't that just something. I just wanted to let you know that you've made one old lady really happy!
—Yours truly, Gladys

YOU'LL BECOME A TEACHER, A PREACHER AND A LOCAL NEWS FEATURE

While I have been Straw Bale Gardening for a very long time already, it is still exciting to see the faces of people who are just learning about how this revolutionary method actually works. They'll ask a hundred questions, they may even make a few skeptically worded inferences, and like it or not you will become a teacher. Every Straw Bale Gardener becomes a teacher, and the more Straw Bale Gardening you do, the more inspired you get. You will soon advance from teacher to preacher, expounding on all the exciting things you've discovered about using this new method of gardening. It won't be long before someone from the local paper or TV news station shows up to do a feature about your garden. For "in all my years, I've just never seen such a wonderful idea" will become a common refrain. Thus the inspiration for this book. It certainly wasn't something I set out to write, but having retold the story of how to grow a garden in bales a million times finally convinced this farm kid to find a better way to spread the word.

Construction is only seven quick steps. A video of how to construct this bin is also on our website (See Resources, page 172).

1. Pound in one post.
2. Move over so there is ½ inch of space between them and pound in a second post, use one of the boards as a spacer here. Wire the top of the first post to the top of the second.
3. Move to the other end of the board and pound in one post a few inches from the end of the board.
4. Pound in the last post on the other side of the board and again wire the first post to the second.
5. Wrap the wire fence from the post on one side to the outside post on the other side and attach using wire, or if the posts have tabs, simply slide the wire fence into the tabs and hammer the tabs down.
6. Put the last post on the outside of the wire fence on the back side, somewhere near the middle of the fence and attach it.
7. Slide the boards in between the posts all the way to the top of the door.

This is my own $10, ten-minute compost bin. It is also the perfect size, and shape, and has great features that make a compost bin very functional.

Every garden needs at least one compost bin, probably two, and in most cases a third is really required. Once a bin is filled up, it can take three to four months, turning the contents every two weeks, to get "finished" compost. I like to fill one, then shovel the contents into another bin immediately next to it every time I turn it. This takes two dedicated bins, moving back and forth. The third one, also positioned next to the other two, is being filled up in the meantime with 2 to 5 gallons of compost a week that get added to the bin at my house. I use plastic one-gallon pails with lids that seal tightly and carry them out when one gets full. Compost all organic matter that your kitchen produces, including peelings, cores and ends of chopped veggies. Never compost meat, cheese or dairy products, as these will attract rodents to the compost pile. Everything from your garden goes in: trimmings, stems and roots of all kinds, and don't worry about putting "diseased" leaves into the bin, since your compost will heat cycle and the "diseased" leaves will have no viable pathogens that remain when the compost has "finished." You may need to dedicate one bin to composting the remains of your bales at the end of the season. I don't recommend mixing this material with traditional compost, keeping the straw compost cleaner and making it a better material for exclusive use in containers, pots and window boxes.

Plant PROFILES

WHEN YOU'RE CHOOSING THE PLANTS you'd like for your Straw Bale Garden, the first question you should answer is, "What do you like to eat?" Of course, it's always fun to experiment with something you've never bought at the grocery store, too.

There are very few crops that I would caution you against growing in your Straw Bale Garden, but some crops are not very conducive to this method. I don't recommend growing corn; it has such a large root system that only a few plants would physically fit in a bale, and the corn gets so tall it will shade most other plants nearby. The few ears of corn you'd produce are not valuable enough to account for the space it takes to grow it. Also, avoid planting those vegetable crops that grow back from the same root stock year after year, such as asparagus and rhubarb. These crops, once planted, take about 2 to 3 growing seasons to become well established, during which time it is recommended that no harvest be taken so as to allow the plants to develop roots using their leaves as an energy source for root development in the fall. In three years, the only thing left of your straw bales would be a little lump of soil in the garden, so these crops would never be harvested from the raised height of a bale. If you plan to establish a plot of asparagus or rhubarb, however, you can simply put the bale in a location where you want the plants to be long term. Bury about one-third of the bale before you condition it. Once conditioned, plant the asparagus or the rhubarb roots in the prepared bale, and come back in three years to observe that an established plot of said crop is now ready to harvest every year going forward.

On the following pages, you'll find useful information to help you select the best herbs and vegetables for your Straw Bale Garden. We'll take a look at the best way to plant your seeds or transplants, and how to care for your seedlings to ensure that you get the most from your harvest. You'll find recommended cultivars for each plant, and even some ways to prepare your produce in the kitchen. For even more advice on planting and growing your own food, don't forget about your County Extension Service. They've always got great information on the best practices and plants for your area.

BASIL

Basil is a tender perennial grown as an annual. The standard type, sometimes called sweet basil, grows about a foot tall. It has tasty leaves and attractive foliage from early summer to first frost and is pretty enough to be used in containers and in flowerbeds. Small-leaved types make good edging plants. There are varieties that have the taste of cinnamon, lemon and lime.

PLANTING: Basil is very frost-sensitive. Sow seeds directly into the seedbed on top of your bales on day 12 of conditioning. They will germinate quickly and grow fast under the poly covers with an extra warm seedbed. Do not pull back the poly covers until a week after all danger of frost has passed. Space plants 10 to 12 inches apart or slightly less, with 6 plants on an average size bale or three plants in one side of a bale. I like to seed at 5-inch spacing and then use the straw bale greenhouse as a nursery to germinate the seeds, later transplanting every other plant from the straw bale into other areas of my gardens.

CARE: Plants should not be allowed to dry out. Fertilize every 2 weeks with a water-soluble fertilizer. Pinch seedlings to encourage branching and bushy growth. Always cut stems back to right above another set of leaves. Remove flower stalks. Rejuvenate plants by cutting back by about half in midsummer. Basil is generally problem-free, but plants are susceptible to damping off, cold temperature damage, and fungal diseases.

HARVEST: Pick leaves whenever you need them. For long-term storage, harvest leaves just before flowers appear and dry or freeze.

CULTIVARS: 'Large Leaf', 'Genovese', and 'Lettuce Leaf' are good standard types. 'Dark Opal' has purple leaves and 'Purple Ruffles' has ruffled purple leaves. They both make beautiful vinegars and are ornamental enough to use in flower gardens. 'Siam Queen' is also ornamental and a good choice for Thai and Vietnamese cooking. 'Spicy Globe' is an ornamental type that forms a neat, 8-inch globe of small leaves.

HOW TO EAT: Eat fresh in salads or mix with almost any other vegetables, or with different cheeses. Basil is wonderful with tomatoes, and serves as one of the two main ingredients in my favorite roasted tomato basil soup. Fresh pesto will also utilize a lot of basil, which then freezes well, and can be thawed out any time of year and is spectacular served over pasta.

SNAP BEANS

Also called string and green beans, snap beans are available as both bush and pole types. Bush beans grow 1 to 2 feet tall and are grown 5 inches apart in two rows on the bales. Pole beans can grow up to 15 feet tall and wide, require the trellis support, and produce more beans than bush types. Snap beans can be yellow (also called wax beans) or purple. Romano beans have broader, flat pods.

PLANTING: Sow seeds on day 12 of conditioning into the seedbed on top of the bale and keep the seedlings covered by the poly tent until all danger of frost has passed. Seeds will germinate quickly and grow well under the covers. Sow seeds 1 inch deep, 8 inches apart. Bush beans bear heavily but briefly. Plant them in a checkerboard pattern, 12 to 16 seeds per bale total. Planting four seeds every other week until mid-summer will keep you in regular supply of beans beginning in about 60 days. Punch climbing sticks (¼-inch thick, 48-inches tall wooden sticks) into the bale between each seedling on the outside of the bale edges. Lean them toward the center and the beans will climb up the stick and then onto the trellis. The beans planted under the trellis will climb immediately. To extend the harvest, sow successive crops of maybe 4 seeds every week up until 12 weeks before the first expected frost.

CARE: Thin bush beans to 5 to 6 inches spacing with only two rows on a bale one row down each side. Beans have the ability to fix nitrogen from the air, as long as the right bacteria are present. You can treat seeds with an inoculant to make sure the bacteria are present. Beans rarely require additional nitrogen fertilizer but usually benefit from additional phosphorus and potassium. Have the support system in place before planting pole beans. Possible problems include damping off, bean rust, leaf spots, bacterial blights, aphids, beetles, leafhoppers, leafminers and whiteflies.

HARVEST: Pick beans when they are thin and tender, before the seeds swell. Pinch or cut the pods off carefully to avoid uprooting the plant. Pick every few days to encourage plants to produce more.

CULTIVARS: 'Blue Lake' or 'Bush Blue Lake', 'Derby', 'Kentucky Wonder', 'Provider', 'Romano'

HOW TO EAT: Eat beans raw, or steam them for 2 to 3 minutes and try to eat them the same day they are picked. Lightly butter or oil them, sprinkle with kosher salt and fresh cracked pepper, and you'll fall in love with green beans, I guarantee it.

BEETS

Beets are another favorite of many who grow in straw bales. It is an extremely sweet and tasty vegetable that comes in many colors and shapes, with many varieties becoming commonly available.

PLANTING: Plant seeds on day 12 of conditioning, and successively weekly. Seeds should be 1 inch deep and from 3 to 6 inches apart in a checkered pattern.

CARE: Water evenly, fertilize regularly.

HARVEST: Pick them when they grow to the size of a golf ball, and use the young leaves in salads as well.

CULTIVARS: 'Forono', 'Chioggia', 'Pronto', 'Green Top', 'Bikores'

HOW TO EAT: Raw beets are great, but cooked with butter, salt and pepper they are phenomenal. Beets are often cooked and chilled then served cold, or pickled as a relish. Beet juice also has many uses. Pureed beets are a staple of the Russian cultural favorite borscht, or beet soup.

BROCCOLI

With this cool-season crop, the part of the plant that is eaten is the flower head, before the buds open. Modern hybrids produce large center heads and abundant side shoots after the center head is harvested.

PLANTING: Start seeds indoors 6 to 8 weeks before the scheduled plant out date or purchase plants in spring. Transplants can go into the garden on day 12 of conditioning, and should be covered only on very cold nights. Place a cutworm collar around young plants to be safe, but normally they are not a problem in a Straw Bale Garden. Spacing can range from 8 to 18 inches, 4 to 9 plants per bale, depending on the variety and how big you want your central heads to be. A second fall crop can be direct seeded in early summer, right between each of the transplants. Make sure seedlings have plenty of moisture as they go through the summer heat.

CARE: Plants decline in summer heat, so cut off spring plantings and allow fall broccoli seedlings to develop. Fall crops will endure a few light frosts. Leaves may develop a bronze or purplish cast if potassium is lacking. Possible problems are club root, cabbage worms, aphids, and flea beetles. Cabbage worms usually stick to the leaves. If you find them in your heads, simply pick them off or soak the head in strong salt water. The insects will float to the top.

HARVEST: Harvest broccoli while the buds are still tight and before there is any yellow color. Use a sharp knife to cut about 2 inches of the stem with the head. Continue harvesting the side shoots after the central head is cut to encourage more shoots.

CULTIVARS: 'Bonanza', 'Packman', 'Premium Crop'

HOW TO EAT: Eat fresh and raw from the garden, or steam for 2 to 3 minutes and lightly butter or oil and sprinkle with kosher salt and pepper.

CABBAGE

Cabbage is a cool-season crop found in many shapes and sizes and colors, with green, blue-green, and red cultivars available. Leaves can be smooth or wrinkled (savoy). Heads develop in cool weather, so it should be planted as early as possible for a spring crop. Cultivars are available that mature early (50 to 60 days from transplanting), midseason (70 to 85 days), or late season (85 days or more). Late-season varieties are best suited to storage and should be timed for fall harvest. Cabbage is one of the few vegetables that can tolerate light shade. It can also withstand light frost.

PLANTING: Best grown from transplants started 4 to 6 weeks before the target planting date after conditioning, or you can buy transplants. Plant on day 12 of conditioning. Space plants 10 to 20 inches apart, 3 to 5 per bale, depending on the head size. Place a cutworm collar around seedlings just to be safe, but normally they are not a problem in a Straw Bale Garden.

CARE: Side dress with a heavy nitrogen fertilizer 3 weeks after transplanting. Plants like ample potassium; a bronze tinge to the leaves signals a deficiency. Possible problems are black rot, fusarium wilt or yellows, aphids, cabbage loopers, cutworms, cabbage root maggots, flea beetles, and slugs.

HARVEST: Heads can be harvested as soon as they are firm, even if they are small. Use a sharp knife to cut off the heads, leaving as much stem on the plant as possible to encourage the production of a second crop of smaller heads. Plant other crops that mature later in the season around the cabbage so that once it is harvested the under-crop can take over the bale.

CULTIVARS: 'Early Jersey Wakefield', 'Dynamo', 'Stonehead' (green), 'Salad Delight' (red), 'Savoy Ace' (savoy)

HOW TO EAT: Cabbage chopped or shredded into fresh coleslaw is amazing, especially when eaten fresh. Boiled cabbage lightly buttered or oiled with kosher salt and pepper is wonderful as well. Cabbage is a common ingredient in foods of almost every culture on earth. My favorite cabbage derivative is sauerkraut—could that be because I have lot of German ancestry? I also love Kimchi just as much, and how can that be explained?

CARROTS

This root crop comes in the traditional size and shape as well as smaller types called fingerlings. There are also round varieties. Smaller types can be ready to eat in 50 days or so. The frilly foliage of carrots makes them pretty enough to use as ornamental plants in your bale garden. Carrots love the loose environment that the straw bales provide inside.

PLANTING: Direct seed in spring on the 12th day of conditioning, and again in any open sunny spots on your bales throughout the summer up until 10 to 12 weeks before the first fall frost date for a fall storage crop. Sow seeds about ¼ inch deep checkered in 2- to 4-inch spacing, or seed them thicker and thin them later. Snip excess sprouts to 2- to 4-inch spacing. You can make succession plantings every week until midsummer. Seeds can be presoaked in water for 6 hours before sowing to hasten germination, which can take up to 10 days.

CARE: Carrots love the Straw Bale Garden environment. Even the tiniest impediment can cause the root to become stunted or forked, and the inside of the bales is very loose and friable, which carrots love. It is better to cut off extra plants with a pointed scissors when thinning rather than pulling the extra seedlings. Avoid high nitrogen, which can cause roots to branch and become "hairy." Hill potting mix lightly around any carrots that become exposed to prevent the shoulders from becoming green and bitter tasting. Possible problems include blight, aster yellows, damping off, wireworms, carrot rust fly, and leafhoppers. Use row covers to protect against insects.

HARVEST: Begin harvesting as soon as carrots are large enough to use or when they are a good orange color.

CULTIVARS: 'Chantenay', 'Scarlet Nantes', 'Touchon'

HOW TO EAT: Fresh and raw is best, but steamed fresh carrots are wonderful with a light honey glaze, and a little salt and pepper. Fresh carrots make a great lunch in the garden. I use a pocket knife to clean the carrot, but don't cut into it, just rub the blade perpendicular to the carrot back and forth. Light pressure shaves off just the outer skin, and leaves a glistening orange treat underneath.

CHIVES

Chives is a hardy (USDA Zone 3) perennial that is very easy to grow. Plants grow into thick, grasslike clumps 8- to 10-inches tall. All plant parts are edible, but it is usually grown for the green leaves, which have a mild onion flavor. Leaves can be cut throughout the growing season as needed and will grow back quickly. Plants are quite ornamental, especially when the showy purple flowers appear in late spring, and are nice additions to a Straw Bale Garden. Keep the roots covered over winter and transplant in the newly conditioned bales every spring on day 12 of conditioning.

PLANTING: The easiest way to start plants is to get a clump from a friend or neighbor; plants are easily divided at just about any time during the growing season. You can also grow chives from seeds, but germination is slow, so be patient. You really only need one or maybe two large plants to keep you happy throughout the year.

CARE: Chive is a vigorous self-seeder. Pick off flowers when they start to turn brown to prevent having hundreds of seedlings everywhere next year. This also prevents plants from going dormant. Divide clumps every 3 to 4 years to keep plants vigorous. To extend the season, pot up a small clump in fall about a month before the first frost and bring it inside once winter hits. Chive has no serious pest problems and rarely needs additional fertilizer.

HARVEST: Use a sharp knife to cut leaves about 2 inches above the base of the stem once plants have reached a height of 6 inches. If you cut back an entire clump, allow it several weeks to regenerate before harvesting again. Don't cut the stems above 2 inches high because the remaining stalk dies back and then the plant gets littered with long dead stalks.

CULTIVARS: The species *(Allium schoenoprasum)* is usually grown for cooking use. There are some cultivars selected for their showier flowers. 'Forescate' has bright rose-red flowers.

HOW TO EAT: I put chives in many dishes, eggs particularly lend themselves to chives. Snip off a dozen or so stems, then use the scissors to simply snip them into ¼-inch lengths directly into the pan on the stovetop. Skip the washing and dragging out a cutting board and knife. A couple of chive flowers, beautifully colored, make an interesting conversation and wonderful flavor in a quiche, a soup or even on a sandwich. They also make beautiful garnish.

CILANTRO, CORIANDER

When grown for its leaves, this annual plant is called cilantro. When grown for its dried brown seeds, it goes by coriander. Cilantro has very fragrant leaves and stems. The young leaves resemble parsley. Plants grow quickly, eventually reaching about 18 inches in height, and go to seed in about 2 months. It is ornamental enough for a flower garden while green, but not so much once it turns brown. It can take partial shade and it does well in a Straw Bale Garden.

PLANTING: Sow seeds on day 12 of conditioning, ½ inch deep, 6 inches apart, 18 to 24 per bale in checkerboard pattern. Sow a few seeds every couple of weeks until late summer to have a regular supply of leaves. Transplants can be put into the sides of bales as well. Plants dry out easily, so be certain to water regularly.

CARE: Seeds need adequate water to germinate, so keep them moist. Plants will bolt (go to seed) quickly in hot weather, after which the foliage is not as tasty. If you want coriander seeds, allow plants to go to seed. No pest problems.

HARVEST: Pinch off leaves as needed for cilantro. Seeds ripen in late summer or fall; collect them before they fall to the ground for coriander.

CULTIVARS: 'Caribe', 'Slo Bolt', 'Santo', and 'Leisure' all tend to go to seed slower than the species.

HOW TO EAT: Fresh cilantro is a powerful herb that adds a special flavor to many fresh vegetable dishes particularly in Mexican, South Asian and Chinese foods. Cilantro makes salsa and guacamole spectacular. Use dried coriander seeds as a spice often for pickling other vegetables and in some German sausage, while the roots can be used to make curry paste.

CUCUMBERS

This warm-season crop is available as traditional vining plants or in compact bush types. Vines require 6 to 8 feet to sprawl while bush types only require 2 to 3 feet. Vining cultivars produce more fruits per plant, but the bush types bear slightly earlier and are easier to care for and harvest. "Picklers" bear earlier, but only for 2 weeks or less. "Slicers" bear later but produce longer, up to 6 weeks. Both types can be used for eating or pickling when small.

PLANTING: Can be direct seeded on day 12 of conditioning, but start seeds indoors about 3 weeks before the planned planting date (or buy transplants at the garden center) to get an earlier harvest. Extend the harvest by sowing seeds at the same time that you set out transplants. Plant a new seed every two weeks, checkered at 18 inches apart, 5 or 6 per bale, spaced according to the package. Vining types should be trained to climb the trellis and bush cultivars can use the lower part of the trellis or can grow down off the sides of the straw bale.

CARE: Plants need warmth and ample water to produce. Pale foliage indicates a lack of nitrogen and bronzing indicates potassium deficiency. Misshapen fruit is a sign of water stress. Possible problems include anthracnose, mosaic virus, cucumber beetles, aphids, and squash vine borer. Pinch off the growing point (end leaf) once the plant reaches the top of the trellis.

HARVEST: Fruits grow quickly, 3 to 5 inches in a day sometimes, and bearing plants should be checked daily. Pick fruits while they are still small; picklers 3 to 4 inches and slicers 6 to 8 inches. Larger fruits are seedy and bitter; they should go right into the compost bin.

CULTIVARS: 'Northern Pickling', 'Liberty' (pickling); 'Marketmore 76', 'Fanfare' (slicing); 'Salad Bush', 'Spacemaster'

HOW TO EAT: Fresh and raw they are wonderful sliced on a salad, on sandwiches, or cubed and mixed with other vegetables or fruits for a salad. Some have thin peelings and the peelings can be eaten, other varieties are best after they are peeled. Small cucumbers make awesome pickles, dill or sweet. Both are easy to make, and delicious. They also make wonderful gifts for the holidays, because who doesn't love pickles?

DILL

Dill is an annual with tasty leaves from early summer to first frost and seed heads that mature in late summer. It can grow 3 feet or taller when it is happy. The feathery leaves and lacy yellow flowers are attractive midsummer. Dill's delicate foliage and tall flowers make it attractive enough for mixed ornamental plantings, but it does drop seeds prolifically. Black swallowtail butterflies use dill as a larval food.

PLANTING: Start sowing seeds on day 12 of conditioning, and then seed successive crops every 3 weeks to ensure a continuous supply. Plant seeds 6 to 8 inches apart in a checkered pattern, or plant started transplants into the sides of a bale. If you want fresh dill for pickling, sow seeds in late spring. Seeds germinate better with some light, so only cover lightly with planting mix, if at all.

CARE: Dill will tolerate afternoon shade. Dill often does not transplant well. No pest problems.

HARVEST: Pick dill weed as you need it, but do not remove more than one-fifth of the plant's foliage or you will weaken the plant. Harvest flower heads when they are half open and seeds when they are brown. To store, hang bunches upside down in paper bags to catch seeds and dried leaves. Whole leaves can be frozen.

CULTIVARS: 'Dukat', 'Tetra', and 'Superdukat' are slow to bolt. 'Fernleaf' is bushier and has more ornamental foliage.

HOW TO EAT: Dill is great when used fresh in many salads, soups or sauces, but the most common use is for pickles and fish. The slight aniseed flavor is strong in the leaves but even stronger in the seeds. If you are planning to grow cucumbers, then don't forget to put in some dill as well—you can use lots of both when you make jar pickles.

GARLIC

This onion relative grows from a bulb that is divided into cloves. It is very hardy, surviving winters in USDA Zone 2. It is best planted in fall and will take about 8 months from planting to harvest. The two main types are softneck and hardneck. Softnecks, most often found at supermarkets, have pliable stems and store well. Hardnecks have stiff central stems that curl at the top. They are more cold-hardy but do not store as well. You can save some of your largest cloves for replanting the next fall. Do not plant supermarket garlic.

PLANTING: Plant individual cloves directly into a conditioned bale 6 weeks before the first snow, around early October depending on where you are. This bale will need to be started with conditioning two weeks prior to this planting; it will be dedicated to mainly garlic production, so the conditioning timing is based on just this crop.

Plant cloves, pointed end up, 2 inches deep directly in the straw, spaced 5 inches apart in a checkered pattern, about 34 to 40 cloves per bale.

CARE: Cover with planting mix after planting to retain moisture. Apply a second layer of mix once the first layer freezes. Stop watering once the foliage begins to turn yellow or fall over. Cut off flower stalks to encourage bulb development. No pest problems.

HARVEST: Leaves can be harvested and used as you would chives, but don't remove more than a quarter of the foliage at one time. Bulbs can be harvested when about three-quarters of the tops have yellowed. Carefully dig up a couple plants and see if bulbs have well-segmented cloves that are beginning to separate. Spread plants, including roots, in a single layer on a screen in a warm, dry, airy location to dry. After 2 to 3 weeks, when bulbs are dry, remove excess dirt, roots, and tops, leaving 1 inch of stem.

CULTIVARS: 'Rocambole', 'Purple Stripe', 'Porcelain' (hardneck). 'Artichoke', 'Silverskin'(softneck)

HOW TO EAT: I put chopped or minced garlic in almost everything. It is one of the most delicious flavor enhancing additions to any meat dish, and goes exceptionally well roasted with olive oil, and sprinkled with good sea salt. Mash into a paste and use it on toast, squash or potatoes.

KOHLRABI

Kohlrabi has a large bulb with protruding leaves that look like cabbage leaves. They are in the cabbage family, so maybe that makes sense. They grow well in a Straw Bale Garden, and they grow quickly.

PLANTING: Plant seeds on day 12 of conditioning. Seed ¾-inch deep and 9 to 10 inches apart, so 10 to 12 per bale.

CARE: Water evenly. Kohlrabi is a brassica, or cabbage, and suffers with all the same diseases and insects as other brassica family members.

HARVEST: Some varieties can be mature in 6 weeks while others will take double that. Slice them off above the root when the bulb gets to be about the size of a baseball. Succession seeding is great for kohlrabi to spread out the harvest.

CULTIVARS: 'Purple Danube', 'Purple Vienna', 'Kongo'

HOW TO EAT: They can be eaten raw—just peel and eat like an apple—or cooked. They are great cubed and roasted with butter, salt and pepper. They can be puréed or used in soups, or simply shredded or chopped into a slaw. Your dinner guests will gasp at how original your menu is when you serve this vegetable—many have never tasted this delicious and under-used dish.

LEEKS

Leeks are in the same family as onion but are longer and thicker without the larger bulb. The thicker stems are what they are grown for. They are easy to grow, and they love the Straw Bale Garden.

PLANTING: Seeds can be planted directly in the seedbed on day 12 of conditioning, or seedling transplants can be purchased. Space either at 6 inches apart; seeds go 1 inch deep, while transplants can go directly in the straw without the planting mix.

CARE: Water evenly and fertilize regularly. Pile planting mix in between the plants when they get to 12 inches high and thicken. The planting mix will help blanch the stalks and allow you to keep them late into the fall. Leek rust is a fungus that can turn the leaves orange. Remove them, but the leeks are probably still fine to eat. Similar pests to onions.

HARVEST: Leeks don't store well so harvest them when you need them. Leave later plantings covered with planting mix late in the fall and early winter until you need them.

CULTIVARS: 'Upton', 'St. Victor', 'Mammoth 2', 'Longbow.' Early varieties tend to be better with whiter stems and are more tender.

HOW TO EAT: Leeks can be eaten raw. With a mild onion flavor, they are great on sandwiches. A popular use is in soups or to flavor stock, boiled or fried. Be sure to chop them up because the long fibers are hard to chew if chunks are left too long.

LETTUCES

The most popular types of lettuce for the home garden are leaf, butterhead, and romaine. Romaine lettuces need a longer growing season but are heat-resistant and can tolerate summer temperatures. Leaf and butterhead lettuces like the cool conditions of late spring and early fall, but modern breeding has produced cultivars that are "bolt-resistant," meaning they are slow to go to seed, and have extended the season for these lettuces.

PLANTING: The small seeds should be carefully scattered on the surface of the seedbed and pressed lightly into the planting mix. They need light to germinate. Sow seeds on day 12 of the conditioning process, and again in mid- to late summer for a fall crop. Make successive sowing every 10 days to extend your harvest. Depending on variety the spacing will be from 2 inches to 18 inches apart, so read the seed pack. You may have from 6 to 60 plants per bale. The paper towel seed tape works well for lettuce, just plant one or two short strips every ten days, with a mix of seeds spaced out properly.

CARE: Lettuces require an even supply of water. Plants will benefit from regular applications of nitrogen. Once hot weather arrives, most lettuces will bolt and need to be ripped out. Lettuces are essentially safe from most insects and diseases. Rabbits are particularly fond of the lettuces. Other possible problems include damping off, downy mildew, mosaic virus, fusarium wilt, aphids, leaf miners, leaf hoppers, slugs, and wireworms.

HARVEST: Begin harvesting leaves as soon as they are large enough. Use a sharp scissor or knife and begin cutting from the outside of the plant first. Pick head lettuces when firm and fully formed. Bigger is not always better, so pick them when you're ready.

CULTIVARS: 'Oakleaf', 'Lolla Rossa', 'Black-Seeded Simpson' (leaf lettuce); 'Buttercrunch' (butterhead); 'Little Gem' (romaine)

HOW TO EAT: Fresh-cut lettuce in a mixed greens salad, with a homemade vinaigrette dressing—nothing tastes better. Don't forget a dusting of salt and pepper. I have become fond of lettuce wraps, which can be a great way to substitute healthy lettuce leaves for high carb bread in normal sandwiches or pitas.

MELONS

Muskmelons are vining plants native to tropical areas. They will do well in northern gardens as long as you select short-season varieties and give plants a head start in your straw bale greenhouse. Start seeds 3 to 4 weeks in advance of your target planting date or buy transplants. Muskmelons have netted skins and salmon, white or green flesh. Other melons, such as cantaloupes, honeydews and watermelons, take longer to mature and are not well-suited to colder climates.

PLANTING: Plant seeds directly into the seedbed on day 12 of the conditioning process, 18 to 24 inches apart, 3 or 4 per bale. In addition, plant a couple of transplants, making sure the poly covers are in place as melons are very sensitive to cold. Plants produce anywhere from two to five melons that usually ripen about the same time. Since plants don't store well, don't plant more than you can enjoy or give away. A few more seeds each week for the next couple of weeks should stagger your harvest and still give them time to mature completely. Plants can be trellised, but you'll need to provide support for each melon. It works well also to let the melons grow partially on the wire and partially on the ground. Pluck the flowers off the trellised vine and let the other part of the same plant on the ground grow the fruits.

CARE: Melons do well planted in the warm bales. Possible problems do include mildews, leaf spots, fusarium wilt, cucumber beetle, aphids, squash bugs, and flea beetles. Floating row covers and proper growing conditions deter diseases and insects.

HARVEST: Muskmelons will "slip," or separate, from the vine when they are fully ripe. To avoid overripening the fruits, harvest when just a little pressure on the stem separates it from the fruit.

CULTIVARS: 'Athena', 'Burpee Hybrid', 'Earli-Sweet'. If you want to try a watermelon, select an "icebox" type such as 'Sugar Baby'.

HOW TO EAT: Peel and slice a fresh melon into chunks for breakfast, lunch and dinner. Melons go very well with a couple drops of aged balsamic vinegar and a sprinkling of sea salt.

ONIONS

Onions are day-length sensitive, with different types requiring different amounts of light and dark to form bulbs. Northern gardeners should choose long-day onions to ensure success. Onions like cool temperatures in the beginning, but require warmer temperatures for the bulbs to mature. Onion colors can be white, yellow, or red and are also classified by their use: storage, slicing, pearl, and scallions or green onions.

PLANTING: Onions are usually planted as sets, which are smallish dormant bulbs, but they can also be started from transplants. Seeds usually take too long to mature when planted outdoors, and seeds are challenging to start indoors. Sets can be planted on day 12 of conditioning. Gently push the onion set into the straw bale surface, with the pointed end up, so that you can just see the top of the set. Space sets 2 to 6 inches apart in a checkered pattern, depending on the mature bulb size, you'll get 24 to 60 onions per bale. Scallions can be planted an inch apart.

CARE: Onions are shallow rooted and require an even supply of moisture. Possible problems include damping off, downy mildew, pink root, smut, onion maggots, thrips, and wireworms.

HARVEST: Harvest scallions as soon as the tops are about 6 inches tall. Bulbs can be pulled as soon as they're big enough to use. Storage onions must stay in the ground until their tops die back and fall over. After harvesting, spread onions in a single layer for 2 to 10 days to cure.

CULTIVARS: 'Stuttgarter', 'Sweet Sandwich', 'Yellow Sweet Spanish' (bulbing). 'Tokyo Long White', 'White Lisbon' (scallion)

HOW TO EAT: Fresh onions are wonderful in many salads or mixed with other vegetables. Onion soup is one of my wife's best recipes. Onions can be roasted, fried, or deep fried, and often serve as the base for many recipes, including meat dishes. Onion rings are a favorite treat, while not the best for your diet. A raw onion slice adds something special to a hamburger, but will keep everyone from kissing you for a while.

OREGANO

This attractive, shrubby perennial is reliably hardy in USDA Zone 5 but often survives winters in Zone 4. It can be grown as an annual in colder climates. Plants have gray-green leaves and loose clusters of purplish-pink flowers in summer. Not all plants have aromatic, tasty leaves, however. The best type for culinary use has white flowers and will have the botanical name *Origanum vulgare spp. hirtum* or *O. heraceloticum* and is usually sold as Greek or Italian oregano. Taste a leaf or two before you buy a plant to make sure it has good flavor. It is quite ornamental and can be used in flower gardens as an ornamental. Marjoram is related to oregano but is more frost-tender and must be grown as an annual.

PLANTING: Start with nursery-grown plants and plant directly in the bales on top or in the side, on day 12 of the conditioning process. Keep the poly covers handy until well after all danger of frost have passed. Space plants at least 12 inches apart, but two or three plants should serve a plentiful supply to even the busiest kitchen.

CARE: Place this perennial herb in a spot where it can be left alone over winter with some protection, and transplanted the following spring into a newly conditioned bale. Its only requirement is full sun, and it does very well in a Straw Bale Garden. Once established, oregano is easy to grow, drought-tolerant, and trouble-free, but you'll want to watch for spider mites.

HARVEST: Leaves are most flavorful before plants flower. Pick leaves as soon as the plant is large enough to be harvested. You can also cut back entire plants when they are about 6 inches tall, again just before they begin to flower, and a third time in late summer.

CULTIVARS: 'Compactum' stays 2 to 3 inches tall and has good flavor.

HOW TO EAT: Fresh leaves can be pinched off and used as flavoring in tomato-based recipes. Many Italian favorites benefit greatly from the oregano flavor profile. Oregano is also lovely used on meat, especially grilled chicken, lamb and fish. Dry the leaves and keep them in a sealed jar where they will stay tasty for at least a year.

PARSLEY

Parsley is a biennial grown as an annual. It has tasty leaves early summer to early winter and attractive bright green foliage all season. It is a larval food source for swallowtail butterflies. Flat-leaved parsley is also called Italian parsley. Curly parsley is often used for garnish.

PLANTING: Parsley grows best in cool weather. Sow seeds on day 12 of the conditioning process. Sow seeds ¼ inch deep and 8 to 9 inches apart, 10 to 14 per bale. Use care if transplanting, as these taprooted plants resent being disturbed. Transplants can be plugged into the sides of the bales. Store seeds overnight prior to planting them out in warm water to speed up germination, which can take 3 weeks. Cover seeds, since darkness aids germination. Mark the seed locations with a popsicle stick because they take so long you may forget where you've planted them. Plant seeds every other week for the first 6 to 8 weeks in the garden, to extend your fresh supply until winter.

CARE: Parsley grows best in full sun, but it tolerates partial shade. It grows well in a Straw Bale Garden. Thin seedlings to 8 inches if you've overplanted. Parsley is tolerant of spring and fall frosts. Usually problem-free, but watch for crown rot. Try to plant enough to share with the large parsley worms, which turn into swallowtail butterflies.

HARVEST: Plants mature 2 to 3 months from sowing. Harvest leaves by cutting rather than pulling, as soon as they are large enough to use.

CULTIVARS: The species (*Petroselinum crispum* Neapolitanum group) is fine for garden use. 'Pagoda' and 'Plain Italian' are good flat-leaved cultivars. 'Sherwood' is a curly-leaved type (*P. crispum* Crispum group) with good heat resistance.

HOW TO EAT: Eat parsley fresh in salads, in soups, on meats, with rice and in sauces and gravies. Parsley also helps freshen breath after eating onions, garlic and other odiferous foods, so is it really a garnish or simply a suggestion?

PARSNIPS

Parsnips are a favorite of many Straw Bale Gardeners, and the easy to grow vegetable has lots of great characteristics that make it delicious.

PLANTING: Direct seed into the seedbed on day 12 of conditioning, lightly covering the seeds spaced 4 to 9 inches apart, or 12 to 24 per bale, depending on the variety. Mark each seed, as they tend to be slow to germinate. Succession seeding is popular to keep the harvest steady.

CARE: Water evenly, fertilize regularly but lightly. Carrot fly and Parsnip canker, which is a fungus affecting the roots, can be problems, but are limited because of the straw bale environment.

HARVEST: Most mature in 14 to 18 weeks, but many like to leave them until after the first hard frost, as it seems to sweeten the flavor somewhat. In all but the coldest areas they can be left in the bales with some protection and harvested throughout the winter.

CULTIVARS: 'Tender and True', 'Andover', 'Gladiator', look for bolt-resistant smooth skin selections.

HOW TO EAT: Parsnips can be eaten raw but are better when cooked. Sometimes they are used to flavor soups or stews and removed after leaving behind some starch for thickening. Boil them, roast them or slice thinly and fry them.

PEAS

Garden peas are grown for their seeds and must be shelled. Snow peas are harvested before the seeds mature and both pods and seeds are eaten. Snap peas have plump sweet seeds and tender pods, both of which are eaten. Vines range from 1 to 8 feet in length; smaller types can be grown without support. Pea flowers are quite ornamental and plants can be used as ornamental flowers.

PLANTING: Direct seed on day 12 of conditioning, into the seedbed of planting mix. Seeds should be planted 1½ inches deep and about 2 to 3 inches apart in two rows, one on each side of the bale. Push ¼ inch x 36 inch-long pea sticks into the bale between every other seed, tipping the sticks toward the trellis. The vines will climb the sticks up to the trellis. Put supports in place at the same time you plant the seeds. Dogwood branches work well for this, or any long straight branches you have available. Plant a few seeds every week for six weeks to spread out the harvest. Plant seeds again in late summer for fall harvest.

CARE: Plants benefit from supports. It makes harvest easier and improves air circulation. Use the wire trellis with sticks or strings, or simply stick a row of branches in the bale for the peas to grow up into. Generally free of insect pests, but watch for blights, wilts, powdery mildew, and root rot. Birds will pull up seedlings to get the seeds.

HARVEST: Pods are usually ready to harvest about 3 weeks after plants flower. Use a small pair of scissors to cut off the pods. Garden peas should have filled pods and still be bright green, not dull. Snow peas can be picked as soon as the pod is full-sized but before the seeds begin to swell. Snap peas should be picked after the seeds have filled out but before the pods are large and hard. Harvest daily.

CULTIVARS: 'Knight', 'Maestro', 'Green Arrow', 'Wando' (garden); 'Mammoth Melting Sugar', 'Oregon Sugar Pod' (snow); 'Sugar Snap', 'Sugar Ann' (snap)

HOW TO EAT: Start the water bath or steamer, then go to the garden and pick the peas. Fresh is key with peas, because shelled peas start loosing flavor the second they are picked. Try to eat what you harvest the same day. Pea soup is spectacular, but peas go wonderfully in many salads as well. Fresh peas with light butter, sprinkled with sea salt and fresh cracked pepper, are really hard to beat. Peas do freeze well, but I'm guessing most won't make it that far. Once your family tastes garden fresh peas, they will be best sellers at your house.

BELL PEPPERS

Most bell peppers start out green and turn red or orange when mature, but there are also yellow, purple, and even brown cultivars. In addition to bell peppers, you can grow jalapeno, Serrano, and poblano types for use in Mexican cooking. All peppers like warm weather, so choose short-season cultivars for best results. Peppers do very well in a Straw Bale Garden.

PLANTING: Start seeds indoors 8 to 10 weeks before the target planting date or buy transplants. Plants cannot be direct seeded. Plant transplants 12 to 18 inches apart into the bale on day 12 of the conditioning process. Keep the poly covers in place until all risk of frost has passed.

CARE: Plants need a constant supply of moisture. Tall types may need support, be sure to get stakes in place before planting to avoid damaging the shallow roots or allow the plants to climb between and around the wires on the wire trellis. Plants usually don't need additional nitrogen. Narrow leaves with a grayish cast are a sign of phosphorus deficiency. Plants also require adequate magnesium. Problems include tobacco mosaic virus, bacterial leaf spot, blossom end rot, sunscald, aphids, flea beetles, cutworms, and tomato hornworms.

HARVEST: Keep plants picked to extend the harvest. They can be picked at the immature green stage or allowed to ripen to their next color. Hot peppers can be picked green, but they will continue to increase in flavor and heat as they mature. Use a pair of scissors to cut fruits from plants. If frost is forecast, pick all remaining fruits.

CULTIVARS: 'Ace', 'Gypsy', 'Northstar', 'Lady Bell' (ripening to red); 'Sweet Chocolate' (ripening to brown); 'Golden Bell' (ripening to yellow)

HOW TO EAT: Fresh raw peppers are tasty in salads, or vegetable mixes. I also love them sautéed in olive oil, with onions and mushrooms. Stuffed peppers are fantastic, baked in the oven with a variety of vegetable or meat stuffing variations. Hot peppers are great for pickling or using fresh as well. Use caution when handling the seeds of hot peppers. Don't touch your eyes or mouth or you can end up at the emergency room. One of my favorite vegetables for part of a grab and go lunch, a raw green pepper is very tasty.

POTATOES

Potatoes require quite a bit of space, so three per bale is about max capacity. Of all the vegetables you'll grow in bales, the biggest labor-saving crop is potatoes. The taste of homegrown potatoes is wonderful, and since growing them in bales is so much easier than in the soil, you really should try some. Choose a variety based on the season of maturity and how you want to use them. Early types are ready to dig about 65 days after planting, midseason about 80 days, and late 90 days or more. Early potatoes are best eaten soon after harvest, while mid and late potatoes are better for storage. Fingerlings are smaller in size and are usually mid- to late season cultivars.

PLANTING: Potatoes are not grown from seeds or plants, but rather small whole potatoes or pieces, called seed potatoes. Purchase disease-free certified seed potatoes from a garden center or nursery near you. On day 12 of conditioning, push the seed potato into the straw bale to a depth of 10 to 12 inches; three per bale is the max. The potatoes form inside the bale. The vines may grow out the top or the sides of the bales. The vines may use the trellis or fill the area in the rows between the bales.

CARE: Potatoes do best in cooler temperatures. The main pest problem is the Colorado potato beetle. Other problems include blights, mosaic virus, wilts, flea beetles, aphids, cucumber beetles, cutworms, Japanese beetles, leafhoppers, and wireworms. Floating row covers will greatly reduce pest problems. Few pests in the Straw Bale environment cause problems with potatoes.

HARVEST: Harvest early types when still small, 7 to 9 weeks after planting, and main crops after the tops have died back but before a hard frost. Simply pull the bale apart and gather your potatoes. They will be very clean when harvested from the bales, which is nice. Try to avoid damaging the tender skins. It is usually better to harvest an entire plant, but you can pluck a few potatoes from several plants. Potatoes to be stored should be cured by spreading them in a single layer in a dark, cool place for 2 weeks.

CULTIVARS: 'Carola', 'Yukon Gold', 'Kennebec', 'Norland', 'Pontiac'

HOW TO EAT: Potatoes should be cooked, or they don't taste good. They can be boiled, baked, fried, deep fried, steamed, grilled or wrapped in foil and thrown into the hot coals of a campfire for 30 minutes. Potatoes are a staple of many cultures and can be a daily source of nutrition for many. The lowly, but tasty, potato is probably the most popular of all vegetables.

RADISHES

This cool-season root crop is very easy to grow. There are several colors and types. The most familiar is the red globe, or spring radish. These grow quickly and are often ready for the table in a month or less. Long-season, or winter, radishes include the Asian radishes (daikon, Oriental, Japanese, Chinese, and lo bok). These are larger and take 2 months or more to reach full size.

PLANTING: Sow seeds on day 12 of conditioning. Plant the seeds ½ inch deep, and about 2 inches apart, 60 or more per bale. Make successive sowings every week until weather is consistently above 65°F. Because spring radishes mature so quickly, they are perfect for intercropping with slower-maturing vegetables. Seeds can be sown again in late summer for a fall crop. Long-season radishes should be planted in spring or summer depending on the cultivar. Winter-storage types should mature around first frost. This is a great crop for kids, who have a short attention span, to grow. Some kids will love the raw flavor, others will hate it, but they will all remember growing something themselves, from planting to harvesting, and finally eating.

CARE: Thin seedlings to 2 to 4 inches or you won't get nice round globes. Maintain even moisture. Water-stressed plants can get bitter and tough. You shouldn't need additional fertilizer with this quick crop. Few problems, but watch for club rot, cabbage root maggots, and flea beetles.

HARVEST: Begin pulling spring radishes as soon as they are large enough to use. Their quality quickly goes downhill as they get large. Winter types can be harvested as soon as they are large enough to use, but a mild frost or two will improve their flavor.

CULTIVARS: 'Cherry Belle', 'Champion', 'White Icicle', 'April Cross', 'Red Meat' (spring types); 'April Cross', 'Misato Rose' (long season)

HOW TO EAT: Fresh raw radishes are a treat. Sliced radish is excellent on a sandwich or in a salad but they can also be cooked or pickled. Roasted radishes with butter and salt have a remarkably great flavor and texture.

RUTABAGAS

Rutabagas are a great vegetable to grow in bales, and a favorite of many. They are in the brassica family, so have some of the same pests. They are globe shaped and about 6 to 8 inches in diameter. Also known as "neeps" in Scotland, and a favorite of Burns Supper revelers in conjunction with haggis. If you don't know Robert Burns, you don't know what you are missing. He is the author of my favorite poem, "To a Mouse."

PLANTING: Seed directly into the seedbed on day 12 after conditioning, and successively to stagger harvest. Seeds are planted ¾ inches deep and 8 to 10 inches apart for 10 to 14 per bale.

CARE: Water evenly, fertilize regularly. Because rutabagas are members of the brassica family, they can suffer pests and diseases similar to cabbage and other members.

HARVEST: Dig them when they mature but before they get "woody" around the tops. They store well packed in sand.

CULTIVARS: 'Ruby', 'Invitation', 'Marian'

HOW TO EAT: Scandinavian cooks rely heavily on rutabagas. They are a key ingredient in soups and casseroles, or thinly sliced and eaten raw. They are great when baked or boiled, and they are commonly served mashed with potatoes or carrots. Delicious, but not flashy, rutabagas are a "workhorse" vegetable.

SAGE

Sage is a hardy (USDA Zone 4) perennial with tasty leaves from early summer to early winter. The textured, gray-green foliage is attractive all season. Culinary sage is Salvia officinalis. There are many other plants that have "sage" as part of their common name but are not suitable for culinary use. Pineapple sage (S. elegans) is a tender perennial with pineapple-scented leaves that can be used in the kitchen.

PLANTING: Plant transplants into bales on day 12 of conditioning. Keep poly covers on until after all danger of frost has passed.

CARE: Sage will grow very well in a Straw Bale Garden. Sage is tolerant of partial shade and drought once established. In colder areas where sage doesn't overwinter, grow plants against a south-facing wall for protection or take cuttings in late summer to be overwintered indoors. Space sage 12 to 24 inches apart, with 3 to 6 per bale. Provide winter protection and transplant into a newly conditioned bale in the spring. Cut plants back by one-third each spring to promote new growth. Even though garden sage is a perennial, plan to replace the woody plants every 3 to 4 years to keep them healthy and vigorous. No serious pest problems but root rot can be a problem.

HARVEST: Pinch leaves off as needed, but stop in early fall to harden plants for winter. For storage, dry leaves in a single layer in a dry location out of sunlight.

CULTIVARS: There are several cultivars that have showier leaves, including 'Aurea', 'Kew Gold', 'Tricolor', and 'Purpurea', but they are not as hardy.

HOW TO EAT: Sage leaves are often used for their strong aromatic character in stuffing, meat dishes or in sauces.

SPINACH

This cool-season leafy green comes in two general types: smooth-leaved or savoyed. Smooth types have thin, tender leaves that are good for salad use. Savoyed types have broader, thicker crinkled leaves and hold up better in cooking.

PLANTING: Sow seeds directly in the seedbed on day 12 of conditioning. Seeds should be planted ¾-inch deep, and 3 to 6 inches apart, with 16 to 30 plants per bale. Sow seeds every 2 weeks in spring to get a continuous harvest and then start again in late summer for a fall crop.

CARE: Thin seedlings to 6 inches, using the thinnings for salads. Spacing that is too tight can lead to bolting, so give plants ample room. These plants usually don't require supplemental fertilizer. This quick-maturing crop is good for succession planting.

Plants will bolt when day length gets over 12 hours or they are exposed to extremely high or low temperatures. No serious pest problems. Blight, downy mildew and fusarium wilt may show up, and plants may be bothered by aphids, flea beetles, leafhoppers and leaf miners. Row covers go a long way in reducing insect damage.

HARVEST: Spring spinach is usually harvested by picking the entire plant before it bolts, but you can cut individual leaves at any time, starting with the outside leaves and moving inward. Fall crops can be harvested either way.

CULTIVARS: 'Tyee', 'Bloomsdale Long Standing', and 'Correnta' are all slower to bolt.

HOW TO EAT: Spinach leaves are spectacular in a mixed greens salad, or "melted" into an omelet. Spinach is a versatile leaf, with lots of nutritional value. Use spinach in many ways, even in your juicer!

SQUASHES & PUMPKINS

Summer squash is picked while immature and the skins are still tender. They generally grow on bushy plants that produce many fruits. Winter squashes and pumpkins are left on the vine until they are mature and have tough, firm skins. They usually grow on long vines with only a few fruits per plant.

PLANTING: Plant transplants directly into the bales on day 12 of conditioning. Two per bale is the maximum, while other early maturing crops can also ride on the same bale. Keep the poly covers handy if any possibility of frost still exists. Squashes love warm temperatures and are easily nipped by frosty temps.

CARE: Plants need plenty of room. Adequate spacing reduces disease problems. Small-fruited plants can be trained on the trellis, but this isn't a good idea for these heavy-fruited plants. Train half the vine up on the trellis and half on the ground. Pluck the flowers on the trellis and allow those on the ground to actually grow fruits. Squashes are heavy feeders, so plan to top dress with a low-nitrogen fertilizer. They also need a regular, plentiful water supply. Potential problems include aphids, cucumber beetle, leaf hopper, squash vine borers, anthracnose, bacterial wilt, mildews, mosaic and scab.

HARVEST: Begin picking summer squashes as soon as they are large enough to use. Winter squashes should be full-colored with skins tough to pierce with a thumbnail; pick all before a hard frost.

CULTIVARS: 'Gold Rush', 'Burpee Hybrid', 'Sunburst' (summer); 'Ambercup', 'Table Ace', 'Sweet Mama', 'Buttercup', 'Blue Hubbard', 'Blue Ballet', 'Cream of the Crop' (winter); 'Howden', 'Lumina', 'Connecticut Field', 'Big Max', 'Ghost Rider', 'Triple Treat' (pumpkins)

HOW TO EAT: Squash can be peeled and cubed, roasted, buttered and served with salt and pepper for a delicious meal. Pumpkins are often grown for the decorative value as jack-o-lanterns but can also be eaten. Making pumpkin pie or dessert is a common use for the unique flavors that pumpkins have.

STRAWBERRY

Strawberries are a hardy perennial for most climates, however they are very prolific growers and will begin to produce almost immediately when transplanted early into a Straw Bale Garden. Strawberries spread veraciously via runners and can be planted as either bare root or plug-type seedlings. The cultivars are varied in size, shape, color, flavor and season of production. Planting early into the warm bales allows for quick establishment and early season production of June-bearing varieties. Strawberry plants can be left in the bales to overwinter and then be transplanted into newly conditioned bales early the following spring. Keeping the poly covers in place early also helps them establish quickly.

PLANTING: Strawberries are among the first plants to go into the garden and can be planted immediately once the bales have completed the conditioning process. Transplants of most cultivars are planted on 12 to 18 inch spacing or 8 to10 plants per bale. The entire surface and sides of the bales can be covered with new plants within a few short weeks.

CARE: Regular fertilization during the growing season is advised with a balanced fertilizer. Several insects and diseases are known to infest the over 200 known cultivars; however, most of these are lessened due to the straw bale growing environment. Full sun and good airflow are important to keep leaves dry and prevent development of fungus and leaf molds. Watch for slugs or other pests.

HARVEST: Pick all berries immediately when fully ripened. The season for ripe berries will vary from spring to late fall. Fruits will turn an even red color, and will tend to attract pests if left to over ripen. Daily harvesting is a must in season.

CULTIVARS: 'Symphony', 'Rhapsody', 'Pegasus', 'Hapil'

HOW TO EAT: Eat them fresh in the garden or in salads or deserts. A favorite of many cultures, strawberries are known to have many health benefits in that they are a terrific sources of vitamin C and flavonoides. Strawberries are also commonly used as flavoring in many other food items, particularly with dairy products. They freeze well and are often used in preserves and can be dried as well.

THYME

There are many types of thyme available for garden use. Most cooks prefer common thyme (*Thymus vulgaris*), which is a shrubby plant growing 12 to 18 inches tall. This hardy (USDA Zone 4) perennial has tasty leaves early summer to fall and attractive foliage all season. Tiny pink flowers appear late spring into summer. These attractive plants can be ornamental as well.

PLANTING: Thyme plants can be planted directly in the bales on day 12 of conditioning. They can tolerate light spring frosts. Thyme is difficult to start from seeds, but plants do very well in a Straw Bale Garden. In colder areas, where garden thyme doesn't always overwinter, grow plants against a south-facing wall for extra protection or take cuttings in late summer to be overwintered indoors. Space plants 6 to 12 inches apart, for 8 to 14 per bale, maximum depending on variety.

CARE: Cut plants back after they flower to encourage bushiness. Cover the plant over the winter and transplant to a newly conditioned bale in the spring. No pest problems.

HARVEST: Cut leaves as needed. Plants benefit from regular shearing. For long-term storage, hang upside down in a dry location out of sunlight. Strip off leaves and flowers and store in a cool, dark place.

CULTIVARS: 'Argenteus' has white-edged leaves. 'Orange Balsam' has orange-scented leaves. 'German Winter' is more compact.

HOW TO EAT: Thyme is a favorite of many chefs and home cooks. Use it fresh or dried, in many soups and stews, or to impart flavor on roasted vegetables or with grilled meats. Can be used as loose leaf if recipe calls for spoonfuls, or left on the branches and used as a tied up bunch to be removed after the flavor has been drawn out.

TOMATOES

Decide first which tomato varieties to grow; choose a variety based on your tastes, your intended use, your available garden space, the length of your growing season and resistance to diseases. Most gardeners grow several types. All do very well in a Straw Bale Garden.

PLANTING: Plant hardened-off plants outside after all danger of frost has passed. Sow seeds indoors 6 to 8 weeks before intended planting date, or buy transplants. Space plants 3 feet apart, so one per bale, two if the varieties are smaller and are not the big hybrid indeterminate vining varieties.

CARE: Plants need even water throughout the growing season; cracked and deformed fruits and blossom end rot are the result of an uneven water supply. They are heavy feeders. Don't over fertilize with nitrogen, however, or you will have all vines and no fruits. All types will grow best if they are staked or caged to get their fruits off the ground. Tomatoes are susceptible to a variety of disease problems, including several wilts, leaf spots, blights and tobacco mosaic virus. Grow resistant cultivars when available and provide optimum cultural conditions. Insect pests include tomato hornworms, aphids, Colorado potato beetles, cutworms, flea beetles, mites, slugs and whiteflies.

HARVEST: Harvest fruits when they are evenly colored and slightly firm or soft. Green fruits will continue to ripen but aren't usually as tasty.

CULTIVARS: 'Tumbler', 'Oregon Spring' (small-fruited types); 'Better Boy', 'Quick Pick', 'Celebrity', 'Lemon Boy', 'Brandywine' (medium-sized fruits); 'Sweet Million' (cherry)

HOW TO EAT: Fresh tomatoes should be immediately sliced and covered with a few shredded basil leaves, drizzled with olive oil and balsamic vinegar, lightly dusted with kosher or sea salt and fresh cracked pepper, spotted with mozzarella or cottage cheese and eaten straight away. By the time winter is over, many would give a whole day's wage for just one really great fresh garden tomato. Freeze fresh tomatoes by first sorting out any with blemished skins or any soft spots. Blanching in boiling water is recommended (to kill bacteria) before freezing. Personally, I never blanch them. I believe that if you sort them well you won't need to worry about bacteria, if they had any bacteria. Once frozen, put your tomato sickles into a reusable plastic bag, and keep them frozen. Whenever a recipe calls for stewed tomatoes, use the frozen ones instead.

TOMATILLOS

Tomatillos, otherwise known as Mexican husk or jamberry tomatoes, are native to Mexico and Central America. The fruits look like small green tomatoes with a paper-like shroud hanging down around them. This husk turns from green to purple to brown and then splits open when it ripens.

PLANTING: Plant seeds indoors 3 to 4 weeks before target planting date or buy transplants to be planted into the seedbed on day 12 of the conditioning process. Keep the poly covers over the top until all risk of frost has passed. Plant them 24 inches apart or 3 per bale. Do not grow just one plant, as they need at least two in order to pollinate properly.

CARE: They will grow about 3 feet tall, and will need the trellis or to be staked. Even watering is essential. No major disease or insect problems. Some similar problems to tomatoes can occur. A long hot summer is great for tomatillos.

HARVEST: Some fruits ripen green or yellow, others purple or red, when paper-like calyx opens and shrivels.

CULTIVARS: 'Toma Verde', 'Verde Peubla', 'Purple Di Milpa'

HOW TO EAT: The fruits taste sweet-and-sour with distinctive tartness that is popular in Mexican salsa and other Latin American sauces. Purple and red cultivars tend to be sweeter and can be used in jellies and jams. They can also be sliced in salads, or on a sandwich or eaten raw.

ZUCCHINI

Zucchini are the rabbits of vegetables, in that they seem to multiply quickly. Really a sister variety of summer squash, it grows very quickly and tastes best when young and tender. Don't plant too many. They can grow from a bump to full size in one or two days, so harvest regularly.

PLANTING: Seed directly on day 12 of conditioning, and successively, but not too often as you'll have more than you can possibly eat when each vine ripens fruits. Plant seeds ¾ inch deep 18 to 20 inches apart or three per bale.

CARE: Water regularly and fertilize occasionally. Not many pests, but cucumber mosaic virus can be an issue.

HARVEST: Start picking when the fruits are no longer than 4 inches and as big as your finger. Harvest them daily or they will go into the compost bin.

CULTIVARS: 'Taxi', 'Milano', 'Gold Rush', 'Bambino'

HOW TO EAT: Grill or roast them with olive oil and kosher salt and pepper. Fantastic flavor and texture, they are a real treat.

Credits

PHOTOS

Photos taken by Tracy Walsh unless otherwise indicated

Photo courtesy the author: pp. 8, 27 (bottom)
Chris Christen: pp. 23 (bottom), 24 (bottom)
Contech Enterprises: page 126
Cool Springs Press: 131 (both), 143
Jen Daugherty: pp. 24 (top right)
John De Franco: pp. 25 (bottom)
William Fleming: pp. 24 (top left)
Sandy Golay: pp. 26 (bottom)
Becky Hoeft: pp. 32 (bottom)
iStock: pp. 51 (top), 56 (bottom), 58 (top), 139, 142 (bottom), 159 (right)
Mark Johanson: pp. 11, 12 (top), 13, 23 (top), 91
Marie Kearns: pp. 22 (top right)
J.J. Lawson: pp. 26 (top)
Crystal Liepa: pp. 98
Paul Markert: pp. 43, 101 (both)
Pascale Marq: pp. 22 (bottom)
Philadelphia Inquirer: pp. 40 (both)
Leslie Proskiw Smith: pp. 25 (top)
Sarah Redding: pp. 27 (top)
Shutterstock: pp. 34, 35, 36 (top), 37 (bottom), 38, 51 (bottom), 55 (bottom), 96, 124, 125, 142 (top), 158, 163, 166 (right), 170 (left)
Lynn Steiner: pp. 155, 156, 157 (right), 161 (both), 162 (both), 166 (left), 167

GARDENS

Mary Young: pp. 18
Mark Johanson: pp. 19 (top)
John Mortensen: pp. 19 (bottom), 20
Kate Clarity: pp. 21 (top and bottom right)
Joel Karsten: pp. 21 (bottom left)
Marie Kearns: pp. 22 (top right)

Resources

STRAW BALE GARDENING

Author (Joel Karsten) website
www.strawbalegardens.com

Straw Bale Gardening Facebook page
Learn to Grow a Straw Bale Garden

PRODUCTS

Page 32
Cedar wood planters that fit a straw bale
www.gronomics.com

Page 33
Find someone with land to share, or gardeners looking for a place to grow.
www.shareddirt.com

Page 38
Straw bales: where to find them
Straw Bale Exchange
www.strawbalemarket.com

Page 64
Bird control
Irri-Tape bird repellent reflective tape
Bird-X
www.bird-x.com
1-800-662-5021

Page 89
Organic fertilizer
Milorganite Organic Nitrogen Fertilizer
www.milorganite.com
1-800-304-6204

Page 126
Motion-activated sprinkler
ScareCrow Motion-activated Animal Deterrent
Contech Enterprises
http://www.contech-inc.com/store/
1-800-767-8658

Page 148
Compost Bin Video

Conversions

METRIC EQUIVALENT

Inches (in.)	1/64	1/32	1/25	1/16	1/8	1/4	3/8	2/5	1/2	5/8	3/4	7/8	1	2	3	4	5	6	7	8	9	10	11	12	36	39.4
Feet (ft.)																								1	3	3 1/12
Yards (yd.)																									1	1 1/12
Millimeters (mm)	0.40	0.79	1	1.59	3.18	6.35	9.53	10	12.7	15.9	19.1	22.2	25.4	50.8	76.2	101.6	127	152	178	203	229	254	279	305	914	1,000
Centimeters (cm)							0.95	1	1.27	1.59	1.91	2.22	2.54	5.08	7.62	10.16	12.7	15.2	17.8	20.3	22.9	25.4	27.9	30.5	91.4	100
Meters (m)																								.30	.91	1.00

CONVERTING MEASUREMENTS

TO CONVERT:	TO:	MULTIPLY BY:
Inches	Millimeters	25.4
Inches	Centimeters	2.54
Feet	Meters	0.305
Yards	Meters	0.914
Miles	Kilometers	1.609
Square inches	Square centimeters	6.45
Square feet	Square meters	0.093
Square yards	Square meters	0.836
Cubic inches	Cubic centimeters	16.4
Cubic feet	Cubic meters	0.0283
Cubic yards	Cubic meters	0.765
Pints (U.S.)	Liters	0.473 (Imp. 0.568)
Quarts (U.S.)	Liters	0.946 (Imp. 1.136)
Gallons (U.S.)	Liters	3.785 (Imp. 4.546)
Ounces	Grams	28.4
Pounds	Kilograms	0.454
Tons	Metric tons	0.907

TO CONVERT:	TO:	MULTIPLY BY:
Millimeters	Inches	0.039
Centimeters	Inches	0.394
Meters	Feet	3.28
Meters	Yards	1.09
Kilometers	Miles	0.621
Square centimeters	Square inches	0.155
Square meters	Square feet	10.8
Square meters	Square yards	1.2
Cubic centimeters	Cubic inches	0.061
Cubic meters	Cubic feet	35.3
Cubic meters	Cubic yards	1.31
Liters	Pints (U.S.)	2.114 (Imp. 1.76)
Liters	Quarts (U.S.)	1.057 (Imp. 0.88)
Liters	Gallons (U.S.)	0.264 (Imp. 0.22)
Grams	Ounces	0.035
Kilograms	Pounds	2.2
Metric tons	Tons	1.1

CONVERTING TEMPERATURES

Convert degrees Fahrenheit (F) to degrees Celsius (C) by following this simple formula: Subtract 32 from the Fahrenheit temperature reading. Then mulitply that number by 5/9. For example, 77°F - 32 = 45. 45 × 5/9 = 25°C.

To convert degrees Celsius to degrees Fahrenheit, multiply the Celsius temperature reading by 9/5, then add 32. For example, 25°C × 9/5 = 45. 45 + 32 = 77°F.

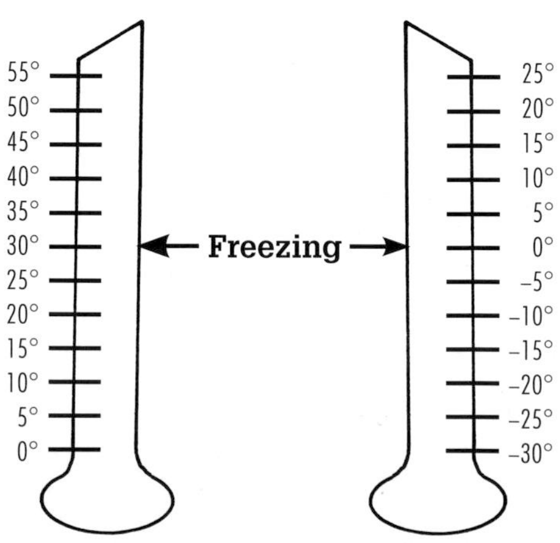

Index

Meet THE AUTHOR

JOEL KARSTEN, a farm boy who grew up tending a soil garden like other gardeners have for centuries, shook up the gardening world with his first book describing his breakthrough Straw Bale Gardening concept. The *New York Times* called Straw Bale Gardening "a revolutionary gardening method" and his ideas have been enthusiastically embraced globally, making his books best-sellers in many languages. Karsten earned a BS in Horticulture from the University of Minnesota and spends his summers tending his vegetable garden, doing research, and experimenting with new ideas and methods he can pass along to his followers. He is a popular speaker, making appearances around the world at events that celebrate innovation, garden enthusiasts and healthful lifestyles, and he is renowned for his social media presence, blog and impressions. Karsten has inspired tens of thousands of first-time gardeners and a legion of "seasoned" growers who found a new and better way to pursue their passion, as well as enabled "retired" gardeners to begin gardening again since his method eliminates the physical challenges found in traditional soil gardening. Discover more information about Karsten and his revolutionary methods at www.StrawBaleGardens.com. Links to his Facebook page, WordPress blog, YouTube Channel, Twitter and Google Plus can all be found on his website.